T0319012

Cambridge Elements ⹀

Elements in Quantitative and Computational Methods for the
Social Sciences
edited by
R. Michael Alvarez
California Institute of Technology
Nathaniel Beck
New York University

INTERPRETING DISCRETE CHOICE MODELS

Garrett Glasgow
NERA Economic Consulting

CAMBRIDGE
UNIVERSITY PRESS

CAMBRIDGE
UNIVERSITY PRESS

University Printing House, Cambridge CB2 8BS, United Kingdom

One Liberty Plaza, 20th Floor, New York, NY 10006, USA

477 Williamstown Road, Port Melbourne, VIC 3207, Australia

314–321, 3rd Floor, Plot 3, Splendor Forum, Jasola District Centre,
New Delhi – 110025, India

103 Penang Road, #05–06/07, Visioncrest Commercial, Singapore 238467

Cambridge University Press is part of the University of Cambridge.

It furthers the University's mission by disseminating knowledge in the pursuit of
education, learning, and research at the highest international levels of excellence.

www.cambridge.org
Information on this title: www.cambridge.org/9781108819404
DOI: 10.1017/9781108873000

© Garrett Glasgow 2022

First published 2022

A catalogue record for this publication is available from the British Library.

ISBN 978-1-108-81940-4 Paperback
ISSN 2398-4023 (online)
ISSN 2514-3794 (print)

Additional resources for this publication at www.cambridge.org/glasgow.

Interpreting Discrete Choice Models

Elements in Quantitative and Computational Methods for the Social Sciences

DOI: 10.1017/9781108873000
First published online: April 2022

Garrett Glasgow
NERA Economic Consulting
Author for correspondence: Garrett Glasgow, garrett.glasgow@gmail.com

Abstract: In discrete choice models the relationships between the independent variables and the choice probabilities are nonlinear, depending on both the value of the particular independent variable being interpreted and the values of the other independent variables. Thus, interpreting the magnitude of the effects (the "substantive effects") of the independent variables on choice behavior requires the use of additional interpretative techniques. Three common techniques for interpretation are described here: first differences, marginal effects and elasticities, and odds ratios. Concepts related to these techniques are also discussed, as well as methods to account for estimation uncertainty. Interpretation of binary logits, ordered logits, multinomial and conditional logits, and mixed discrete choice models such as mixed multinomial logits and random effects logits for panel data are covered in detail. The techniques discussed here are general and can be applied to other models with discrete dependent variables that are not specifically described here.

Keywords: discrete choice, first difference, marginal effect, elasticity, odds ratio

ISBNs: 9781108819404 (PB), 9781108873000 (OC)
ISSNs: 2398-4023 (online), 2514-3794 (print)

Contents

1 Introduction

This Element describes basic techniques for the interpretation of models with discrete dependent variables. All of the models discussed here are applicable to cases where an individual makes a choice from a discrete set of choice alternatives, and for this reason they are often known as *discrete choice* models. However, this theoretical motivation is not required, and the techniques described here can be applied no matter what type of outcome is being analyzed. Throughout this Element I assume the reader has a basic understanding of statistical inference and maximum likelihood estimation, knows how to select the appropriate statistical model for the task at hand, and is able to estimate the model coefficients and standard errors. The goal of this Element is to provide guidance on producing more meaningful interpretations of the model coefficients.

This Element covers three basic techniques for calculating the effects of the independent variables on the choice probabilities: (1) first differences in predicted probabilities, (2) marginal effects and elasticities, and (3) odds ratios. These estimated quantities reveal the magnitude of the effects of the independent variables on the choice probabilities, demonstrating the real-world implications of discrete choice models for both technical and nontechnical audiences. Throughout this Element I refer to these estimated quantities as *substantive effects*. While some of the techniques covered here are also discussed in other treatments of discrete choice models (e.g., Gelman and Hill 2007; Long 1997; Ward and Ahlquist 2018), this Element differs from previous work in several ways. Specifically, this Element (1) describes a broad set of interpretive techniques drawn from political science, economics, sociology, and epidemiology, which have not previously been covered in a single text, (2) demonstrates how to account for statistical uncertainty when using each of these techniques, and (3) demonstrates the use of these techniques for mixed discrete choice models, which have not previously received in-depth coverage at an introductory level.

The models covered in detail in this Element are binary logits, ordered logits, multinomial and conditional logits, and two mixed discrete choice models – random effects logits for panel data, and mixed multinomial logits (often known as mixed logits). The techniques discussed here are general, and can be applied to many other models with discrete dependent variables which are not specifically described, including the probit versions of the models covered here.

All of the models discussed here are of the form $p_{ij} = \text{Pr}(y_i = j|X_{ij}) = F(X_{ij}\beta)$, where p_{ij} and $\text{Pr}(y_i = j)$ are the probability that individual i chooses alternative j from a choice set consisting of J alternatives, $X_{ij}\beta$ is a linear function of independent variables (X_{ij}) and coefficients (β) that describe the individual and/or the choice alternative, and $F(.)$ is a cumulative distribution function (CDF) that translates $X_{ij}\beta$ into choice probabilities.[1] Estimating these discrete choice models produces a vector of estimated coefficients $\hat{\beta}$ and an estimated covariance matrix $\hat{V}(\hat{\beta})$. Unless indicated otherwise, all equations in this Element refer to estimated quantities, which are written without using the "hat" operator (e.g., β instead of $\hat{\beta}$, p_{ij} instead of $\hat{p}_{ij}$, and so on).

While the estimated coefficients and standard errors can (in most cases) be used to determine the direction of the effect of an independent variable on a choice probability (positive or negative), and whether this effect is statistically significant, determining the magnitude of the effect is less straightforward. The effect of an independent variable x on the choice probability is nonlinear, and will depend both on the particular value of x and on the values of the other independent variables.

For example, consider a simple binary choice model $p_i = \Pr(y_i = 1|x_i, C) = F(C + x_i\beta)$, where y is the binary dependent variable (coded 1 for a "success" and 0 for a "failure"), and C represents any other influences on $\Pr(y = 1)$ (such as the constant term and the values of the other independent variables) that are held constant while calculating a substantive effect for x. Figure 1 demonstrates how various 1-unit changes in x produce different changes in $\Pr(y = 1)$, even when β is held constant at 1.[2] Holding $C = 0$, a 1-unit change in x from -1 to 0 increases $\Pr(y = 1)$ by ≈ 0.23, while a 1-unit change from 1 to 2 only increases $\Pr(y = 1)$ by ≈ 0.15 (Figure 1, panel (a)). Changing C from 0 to 1.5 (such as by changing the value of a different independent variable in the model) increases $\Pr(y = 1)$ for all values of x, shifting the probability curve to the left (upwards). This shift changes the effect of a 1-unit change in x from 0 to 1 on $\Pr(y = 1)$ from ≈ 0.23 to ≈ 0.11 (Figure 1, panel (b)). For these reasons, the substantive effects described here are calculated at specific values of the independent variables.

In the following section, I describe several methods for accounting for the statistical uncertainty in estimated substantive effects. I then describe the techniques for calculating substantive effects in some detail in the context of the binary logit. Finally, I extend all of these concepts to the other discrete choice models mentioned above.

---

[1] In the generalized linear model (GLM) framework, this function is the inverse of the link function (McCullagh and Nelder 1989, ch. 2).

[2] The probability curve presented in Figure 1 comes from a binary logit model where $F(.)$ is the CDF of the logistic distribution, but this basic point holds for all of the discrete choice models examined in this Element.

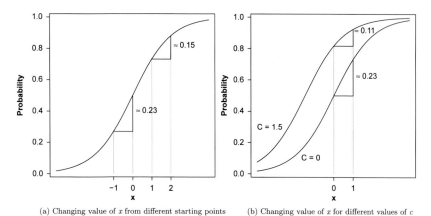

(a) Changing value of x from different starting points (b) Changing value of x for different values of c

Figure 1 Substantive effects of a change in x on the choice probability

The data and code necessary to replicate each example are available through GitHub[3] or Dataverse.[4] The replication code was written using the open-source statistical software R (R Core Team 2021). The use of prewritten packages in the code was minimized – instead, the formulas were written out in "longhand" to reinforce the calculations underlying each method.

2 Accounting for Statistical Uncertainty in Estimates of Substantive Effects

Since the discrete choice model coefficients β are estimated with statistical uncertainty (as evidenced by the standard errors on these estimates), and the substantive effects described in this Element are based on these coefficients, the statistical uncertainty contained in β will carry over to any estimates of substantive effects. In this section, I describe three methods that can be used to account for statistical uncertainty in estimated substantive effects: (1) simulated coefficients, (2) bootstrapping, and (3) the delta method. For other comparisons of these approaches to estimating uncertainty, see Dowd, Greene, and Norton (2014), Hole (2007), and Mandel (2013).

2.1 Simulated Coefficients

The method of *simulated coefficients* takes a large number of random draws from the multivariate normal distribution defined by the estimated coefficients and covariance matrix, and calculates the substantive effect for each of these draws (King, Tomz, and Wittenberg 2000; Krinsky and Robb 1986

---

[3] https://github.com/GarrettGlasgow/interpreting-discrete-choice-models
[4] https://dataverse.harvard.edu/dataset.xhtml?persistentId=doi:10.7910/DVN/0NVMEX

1990). This method is also known as the *Krinsky–Robb* method (after Krinsky and Robb 1986) or the *parametric bootstrap* (Efron and Tibshirani 1994, pp. 53–55).

Under standard maximum likelihood estimation regularity conditions, the estimated coefficients from a discrete choice model will be asymptotically distributed as multivariate normal (e.g., Long, 1997, pp. 85–86; Train 2009, p. 200). The method of simulated coefficients relies on this property, taking D draws from $N(\beta, V(\beta))$, calculating the substantive effect for each draw, and then summarizing the distribution of the substantive effect across the draws. Obviously, the larger the variance terms in $V(\beta)$, the greater the statistical uncertainty in the estimate of β, and thus the larger the variance will be on any substantive effect that relies on β. The number of draws used is typically large ($D = 1000$ or more).

Since the method of simulated coefficients relies on random draws, the results will vary with each new set of draws.[5] This simulation error can be reduced by simply increasing the number of draws – simply calculate the estimation uncertainty in the substantive effects several times, increasing the number of draws each time until the results stabilize such that adding more draws does not produce meaningful changes in the results.

The means and medians of the simulated substantive effects in most cases will be very similar to the value obtained by simply using β – the primary goal of the method of simulated coefficients is to obtain a measure of estimation uncertainty for the substantive effects based on β. One way to do this is to calculate the variance of the D simulated substantive effects, and from there calculate standard errors and confidence intervals. Another approach is to construct confidence intervals from the percentiles of the simulated substantive effects (confidence intervals constructed in this way are often referred to as *percentile intervals*). For example, the lower and upper limits of a 95% confidence interval are given by the 2.5th and 97.5th percentiles of the distribution of the D simulated substantive effects. Calculating percentile intervals relaxes the assumption that the confidence intervals are symmetric. Symmetric confidence intervals may be inappropriate in some cases – for instance, the confidence interval on a predicted probability will likely become asymmetric as the predicted probability approaches the boundary of 0 or 1, with the confidence interval becoming more narrow on the side of the predicted probability that is closer to the bound. Symmetric confidence intervals based on multiples of the standard error of the substantive effect will not capture this asymmetry,

---

[5] This would not be the case if quasi-random draws such as Halton draws are used. Halton draws are discussed in the context of mixed discrete choice models in Section 6.1.

and in some cases can even produce confidence intervals that cross over the bounds (implying probabilities less than 0 or greater than 1).

Applying the method of simulated coefficients to account for estimation uncertainty is computationally fast, and accuracy can be increased by simply increasing the number of draws. Most of the calculations of statistical uncertainty in this Element rely on the method of simulated coefficients. However, there are at least two other approaches to accounting for estimation uncertainty in substantive effects that will produce similar results in most applications, and that are valid choices in most circumstances.

2.2 Bootstrapping

Bootstrapping is the process of generating multiple simulated datasets by resampling from an observed dataset (Davison and Hinkley 1997; Diaconis and Efron 1983; Efron and Gong 1983; Efron and Tibshirani 1994). The most straightforward approach to bootstrapping is to take a number of simple random samples with replacement of size n from the n observations in the original dataset. Simple random sampling means that each observation has an equal chance of being selected as an observation in each simulated dataset, and sampling with replacement means that each simulated dataset will differ from the original dataset (some observations will appear multiple times, while others will be omitted). More complicated resampling schemes are possible.

To estimate uncertainty in a substantive effect using bootstrapping, D bootstrapped datasets are generated, the discrete choice model is estimated for each of these datasets, and the substantive effect is calculated for each of the D versions of the discrete choice model. The distribution of the D simulated substantive effects can then be summarized as described in the previous paragraph. Bootstrapping as described here is sometimes called *nonparametric bootstrapping*, since, unlike the method of simulated coefficients (parametric bootstrapping), it does not rely on the asymptotic normality of the maximum likelihood estimates. Bootstrapping is thus a more conservative choice than the method of simulated coefficients, since it does not rely on any distributional assumptions.

As with the method of simulated coefficients, results obtained through bootstrapping will depend in part on randomness – in this case, the particular random samples that produce the simulated datasets. Again, simulation error can be reduced by recalculating the uncertainty in the substantive effects several times, increasing the number of simulated datasets each time until the results stabilize. The main drawback of bootstrapping is computational time, since the discrete choice model must be estimated for each simulated dataset. The analysis for each simulated dataset in the bootstrap will take approximately as much computational time as the entire analysis using the method of simulated coefficients or the delta method (Section 2.3).

2.3 The Delta Method

The *delta method* is an analytic method that can be used to find the distribution of a nonlinear function of random variables that follow a known distribution (Agresti 2013; Oehlert 1992; Ver Hoef 2012). In this particular case, the random variables are the estimated coefficients β, and the nonlinear function of these random variables is $G(\beta)$, a substantive effect based on the estimated coefficients. Analytically calculating the variance of this nonlinear function is generally so difficult as to be impractical. The delta method solves this problem by creating a linear approximation of the function through a first-order Taylor series expansion.

The estimated coefficients from the discrete choice model are assumed to be asymptotically normally distributed, as described in Section 2.1. With this assumption, the delta method can be used to calculate the analytic variance of the linear approximation of $G(.)$ as:

$$V(G(\beta)) \approx \left(\frac{\partial G(\beta)}{\partial \beta}\right)' V(\beta) \left(\frac{\partial G(\beta)}{\partial \beta}\right), \tag{1}$$

where $\partial G(\beta)/\partial \beta$ is the gradient of the function $G(.)$ with respect to β (that is, the vector of partial derivatives of $G(.)$ with respect to the coefficients on each independent variable) at the maximum likelihood estimates of β. Standard errors on the substantive effect are given by the square root of this calculated variance, and confidence intervals can be constructed from these standard errors in the usual way – for instance, a 95% confidence interval is given by $\pm 1.96 \times \sqrt{V(G(\beta))}$.

The primary advantage of the delta method is speed. In most cases, calculating the statistical uncertainty of a substantive effect using the delta method adds almost no additional computing time to the analysis. However, the delta method is an approximation, and thus will be subject to some degree of inaccuracy. Accuracy can be increased by using higher-order Taylor series expansions, but this can be analytically difficult. In contrast, the accuracy of the simulated coefficients and the bootstrapping methods can be improved by simply increasing the number of draws. Finally, the delta method constructs confidence intervals based on the estimated standard error of the substantive effect, which will produce symmetric confidence intervals that may be undesirable in some circumstances, as described in Section 2.1.

2.4 Example: The Use of Insecticide-Treated Mosquito Bed Nets in Uganda

Malaria imposes a significant health burden on many countries in sub-Saharan Africa. Beginning in 2005, the government of Uganda and several nongovernmental organizations began a campaign to distribute insecticide-treated bed nets (ITNs) across the country in order to reduce the population's exposure to mosquito bites while sleeping. The use of ITNs has been shown to be an effective preventative measure for malaria. Despite this, not all households that own an ITN use it every night. The inconvenience of hanging the net, the discomfort of sleeping under the net (too hot), and the poor condition of the net (too many holes) are commonly cited reasons for not using an available ITN. Additionally, some households that own ITNs divert them to other purposes, such as fishing nets. How to best distribute ITNs and ensure their proper use has become a central topic of debate in the field of international development (e.g., Easterly 2006; Sachs 2005).

The 2014–15 Uganda Malaria Indicator Survey (Uganda Bureau of Statistics 2015) was conducted in part to determine how frequently households that owned ITNs actually used them. The data in this example consist of 5,119 women ranging in age from 15 to 49. This demographic group is of particular interest as they are the respondents most likely to be pregnant or caring for small children (pregnant women and infants are particularly susceptible to malaria).

The dependent variable is y_i, coded 1 if survey respondent i reported using an ITN the previous night, and 0 otherwise. The choice probability for $y_i = 1$ in a binary choice model is specified as $p_i = F(X_i\beta)$, where $X_i\beta$ is a linear function of independent variables X_i and coefficients β, and $F(.)$ is the appropriate CDF. Setting $F(.)$ to the CDF of the standard logistic distribution $\Lambda(.)$ leads to the *binary logit* model (more commonly known as the *logit* model):[6]

$$p_i = \Pr(y = 1|X_i) = \frac{\exp(X_i\beta)}{1 + \exp(X_i\beta)} = \Lambda(X_i\beta). \tag{2}$$

I modeled the decision to sleep under an ITN as a function of several independent variables. Hearing or seeing a malaria-related educational message on the radio, television, billboard or poster, or from a health worker in the six months before the survey (1 = heard message, 0 = did not hear message) was expected to increase ITN use, as these respondents should have been more likely to be aware of the benefits of using ITNs. Higher levels of education

---

[6] Setting $F(.) = \Phi(.)$, the CDF of the standard normal distribution, leads to the *binary probit* or *probit* model.

Table 1 Logit model for use of an ITN

Independent Variable	Coefficient	(se)	95% CI	
Malaria Education Message	0.186	(0.069)	0.050	0.322
Years of Education	−0.031	(0.009)	−0.049	−0.013
Top Wealth Quintile	−0.238	(0.088)	−0.412	−0.065
Bottom Wealth Quintile	0.095	(0.088)	−0.077	0.268
Pregnant	0.040	(0.116)	−0.187	0.267
Altitude of Residence	−0.355	(0.132)	−0.613	−0.097
Constant	1.674	(0.186)	1.310	2.038
Number of Observations	5,119			

(measured in years) and wealth (1 = top quintile in wealth, 0 = otherwise) were expected to decrease ITN use, as these respondents were more likely to live in urban areas with better access to medical care and with higher quality housing (e.g., window screens) that can prevent transmission of malaria. Conversely, respondents in the bottom quintile of wealth were expected to be more likely to use ITNs (1 = bottom quintile in wealth, 0 = otherwise).[7] Women who were pregnant (1 = pregnant, 0 otherwise) were expected to be more likely to use an ITN, since pregnant women are particularly vulnerable to malaria, and are often given additional attention and information during routine medical care. Respondents living at higher altitudes (measured in thousands of meters) were expected to be less likely to use ITNs, as malaria is not endemic to higher altitude areas. Table 1 presents the results from estimating a logit model on these data.

While the substantive effects of the independent variables on p_i are at this point unknown, the directional effect and the statistical significance of the independent variables can be determined from Table 1. Respondents who were recently exposed to a malaria education message were more likely to have used an ITN the previous night, while respondents with higher levels of education, in the top wealth quintile, and in residence at higher altitude were less likely to have used an ITN the previous night. Pregnancy and wealth in the bottom quintile did not have a statistically significant effect on ITN use at the commonly used 5% significance level.

---

[7] The wealth index was constructed from household asset data such as ownership of a television, bicycle, or car, as well as dwelling characteristics such as source of drinking water, sanitation facilities, and type of flooring material.

Now consider calculating a simple substantive effect – in this case, the probability of sleeping under an ITN calculated at the means of the independent variables. This probability is easily calculated by replacing X_i with $\bar{X}$ in Equation 2, and is ≈ 0.784. However, this calculation does not reflect the statistical uncertainty in the estimate of β.

To apply the method of simulated coefficients to this example, I drew 1000 sets of simulated coefficients from $N(\beta, V(\beta))$. Each set of simulated coefficients was then used to calculate the predicted probability at the means of the independent variables. The resulting set of 1000 predicted probabilities was then summarized in order to obtain standard errors and confidence intervals.

To apply bootstrapping to this example, I drew 1000 simulated datasets with the same number of observations as the original dataset (5,119) using simple random sampling with replacement. The logit model specified in Table 1 was estimated for each of these 1000 simulated datasets, and each new set of coefficients was used to calculate the predicted probability at the means of the independent variables calculated using the original dataset. The resulting set of 1000 predicted probabilities was then summarized.

To apply the delta method to this example, I first calculated the gradient of the logit model in Equation 2 at $X_i\beta$:

$$g(X_i\beta) = [\Lambda(X_i\beta)(1 - \Lambda(X_i\beta))]\, X_i = \lambda(X_i\beta)X_i, \tag{3}$$

where $\lambda(.)$ is the probability density function (PDF) of the logistic distribution.

I then substituted $g(.)$ for $\partial G(\beta)/\partial\beta$ in Equation 1, and $\bar{X}$ for X_i in Equation 3 to obtain:

$$V(F(\bar{X}\beta)) = \left(\lambda(\bar{X}\beta)\bar{X}\right)' V(\beta) \left(\lambda(\bar{X}\beta)\bar{X}\right) = \lambda(\bar{X}\beta)^2 \bar{X}' V(\beta)\bar{X}. \tag{4}$$

This estimated variance was then used to calculate standard errors and confidence intervals.

Table 2 presents the results from applying each of these methods of calculating statistical uncertainty to this example. The 95% confidence intervals for the method of simulated coefficients and bootstrapping are based on the 2.5th and 97.5th percentiles of the predicted probabilities, while the 95% confidence interval for the delta method is based on ± 1.96 times the calculated standard error.

All three methods for accounting for uncertainty produced nearly identical results in this example, although this will not always be the case.

Table 2 Uncertainty in the predicted probability of using an ITN

	Median	(se)	95% CI	
Simulated Coefficients	0.760	(0.006)	0.749	0.771
Bootstrapping	0.761	(0.006)	0.749	0.773
Delta Method	0.760	(0.006)	0.749	0.772

Note: Estimates were based on the logit model presented in Table 1, holding all independent variables at their means; 1000 draws were used for the method of simulated coefficients and bootstrapping.

3 Substantive Effects in Binary Choice Models

In this section, I describe techniques for calculating substantive effects for a binary logit model. All of the techniques described in this section apply equally to the binary probit except where noted.

3.1 First Differences

One straightforward way to estimate the substantive effect of an independent variable in a discrete choice model is to calculate the difference between the predicted probabilities at two different values of the independent variable of interest, holding the values of the other independent variables constant. This calculation is commonly known as a *first difference* or a *discrete change*. As Figure 1 demonstrates, the first difference will depend on both the values of the specific independent variable being examined and the values of the other independent variables in the model. In the binary case, selecting values of the independent variables that produce predicted probabilities near 0.5 will produce the largest estimated substantive effects, while selecting values that produce predicted probabilities near 0 or 1 will have the opposite effect (see Figure 1).

Most often a first difference will be based on a change in the value of a single independent variable. However, in some cases it will be more logically consistent to vary the values of more than one variable, most commonly if the independent variable of interest is interacted with another variable, since changing the value of the variable of interest will also necessarily change the interaction term. Changing the values of more than one independent variable in a first difference may also be reasonable if some combinations of values of the independent variables are logically impossible (e.g., Glasgow, Golder, and Golder 2012).

A common approach to calculating first differences is to use *hypothetical cases*, in which the values of the independent variables have been set to specific values that reflect cases of real-world interest or importance. Another approach to calculating first differences is to simply set all independent variables to their means, and then vary the value of a single variable. Medians or modes could be substituted for means in cases that could not exist in the data (the mean of a dummy variable, for example).

For two different sets of values of the independent variables X_A and X_B, the first difference in a binary choice model between case A and case B is:

$$\Delta p(X_A \to X_B) = \Pr(y = 1|X_B) - \Pr(y = 1|X_A). \tag{5}$$

Differences-in-differences (differences between first differences) can also be calculated. For example, in cases where an independent variable is expected to have a larger effect for one group (Group 1) as compared to another (Group 2), the values of the independent variables are set by varying both the independent variable of interest and the variable indicating group membership. This produces four sets of values for the independent variables: X_{A1} and X_{B1} for Group 1, and X_{A2} and X_{B2} for Group 2. The difference-in-differences is then calculated as $\Delta p(X_{A1} \to X_{B1}) - \Delta p(X_{A2} \to X_{B2})$.

Returning to the ITN example presented in Table 1, I calculated the substantive effect of exposure to a malaria education message through a first difference. I first created two different hypothetical cases, one with no exposure to a malaria education message (malaria education message = 0), and the other with exposure to a malaria education message (malaria education message = 1). I assumed that the woman in these hypothetical cases was in the bottom quintile of wealth, was not pregnant, was at the median in years of education, and lived at the median altitude in the sample. I then calculated the predicted probabilities for both hypothetical cases. Statistical uncertainty for each of these predicted probabilities was accounted for using the method of simulated coefficients with 1000 draws. Finally, I calculated the first difference as the difference between the predicted probabilities for these two hypothetical cases. Since I used the method of simulated coefficients, this calculation is simply the difference between the two vectors of 1000 predicted probabilities, with each of the 1000 calculated differences using the same draw of β.

The first three lines of results in Table 3 present the results from the predicted probability and first difference calculations across the 1000 simulated coefficients. As expected, the probability of ITN use increased for this hypothetical individual when she was exposed to a malaria education message. The first difference calculation shows that the probability of ITN use increased by approximately 0.032, and the 95% confidence interval on this change did not include zero, indicating that this increase was statistically significant at the 5% level.

Table 3 First differences in the predicted probability of using an ITN based on wealth and malaria education message

	Median	(se)	95% CI	
Bottom Wealth Quintile = 1				
Malaria Education Message = 0	0.763	(0.017)	0.729	0.794
Malaria Education Message = 1	0.795	(0.013)	0.768	0.819
Malaria Education Message 0 → 1	0.032	(0.012)	0.009	0.056
Top Wealth Quintile = 1				
Malaria Education Message = 0	0.696	(0.019)	0.659	0.733
Malaria Education Message = 1	0.735	(0.015)	0.705	0.765
Malaria Education Message 0 → 1	0.038	(0.014)	0.011	0.067
Difference-in-Differences	0.005	(0.003)	0.001	0.012

Note: Estimates were based on the logit model presented in Table 1. Standard errors and confidence intervals were calculated using 1000 sets of simulated coefficients.

I also considered whether exposure to a malaria education message had a different substantive effect based on wealth. To do this, I created two new hypothetical cases identical to the cases described, except the hypothetical woman was assigned to the top rather than the bottom quintile of wealth. I then calculated predicted probabilities and the first difference using these new hypothetical cases. These results are presented in the next three rows of results in Table 3. As expected from the logit model presented in Table 1, the predicted probabilities show that women in the top wealth quintile were less likely to sleep under an ITN than women in the bottom wealth quintile. The first difference for this new set of hypothetical cases demonstrates that, as with women from the bottom wealth quintile, exposure to a malaria education message had a positive and statistically significant effect on the probability of ITN use for women from the top wealth quintile.

Finally, I calculated a difference-in-differences based on the difference between these two first difference calculations. The method of simulated coefficients with 1000 draws was used to account for statistical uncertainty, so each first difference calculation produced a vector of 1000 probability differences. The difference-in-differences was calculated as the difference between these two vectors, with each difference-in-differences calculated using the same draw of β. This calculation shows that the substantive effect of exposure to a malaria education message on the probability of ITN use was slightly larger for this hypothetical woman when she was in the top wealth quintile as compared

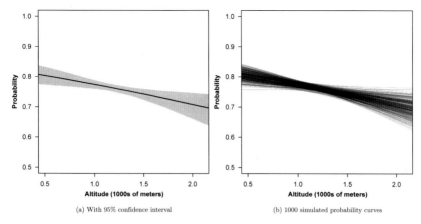

(a) With 95% confidence interval   (b) 1000 simulated probability curves

Figure 2 Probability of using ITN as a function of altitude

to the bottom wealth quintile. Further, the 95% confidence interval on this difference-in-differences did not include zero, indicating that this difference was statistically significant at the 5% level. That is, holding all other independent variables constant at the values specified, exposure to a malaria education message led to a larger increase in the probability of ITN use for women in the top wealth quintile as compared to women in the bottom wealth quintile.

Another example of a first difference calculation is presented in Figure 2. This figure represents the change in the probability of using an ITN as altitude increases, holding all other independent variables at their means. The method of simulated coefficients was used to create 1000 versions of this probability curve. Panel (a) presents the mean probability and 95% confidence interval (calculated from the 2.5th and 97.5th percentiles of the predicted probabilities at each altitude), while panel (b) presents all 1000 predicted probability curves generated from the 1000 sets of simulated coefficients. Both panels are based on the same underlying probability curves, and are simply alternative ways of presenting the same information.

First differences can also be calculated by considering changes in the choice probabilities across the entire sample rather than a single (real or hypothetical) observation. The most common approach is to calculate the predicted population-level share for a choice alternative j. Population-level shares are typically calculated through *sample enumeration*. A consistent estimate of the share of the population that selected choice alternative j is given by:

$$S_j = \frac{\sum_{i=1}^{n} p_{ij} w_i}{\sum_{i=1}^{n} w_i}, \tag{6}$$

where n is the number of observations in the sample, p_{ij} is the predicted proba-bility for individual i for choice alternative j calculated at a given set of values of the independent variables X_{ij}, and w_i are the sampling weights (the recip-rocal of the probability that observation i would have been sampled from the population). In a simple random sample, these sample weights will be identical for all observations and can be ignored, but if some subpopulations are under-sampled or oversampled the weights are necessary for accurate aggregation to the population-level shares. Note that the mean of the individual choice prob-abilities across the sample as given by S_j will generally not equal the choice probability at the means of the independent variables. Calculating population shares by using the means of the independent variables rather than averaging over the individual choice probabilities can lead to *aggregation bias* (Train 2009, p. 29–31). Also note that sample enumeration is based on the sum of the predicted probabilities (an expected value) rather than a sum of predicted val-ues for each observation. While it is possible to calculate predicted values for each observation based on the predicted probabilities (in a binary choice model, this is most often done by assuming $\hat{y} = 1$ if $p > 0.5$),[8] this approach ignores much of the uncertainty in these models by treating all predicted probabilities above or below some threshold as equally certain predictions of choice, and thus the use of predicted values in discrete choice models should generally be avoided (Train 2009, p. 69).

Selecting different sets of values for the independent variables will change the choice probabilities, and thus the estimated shares for the choice alterna-tives. For example, a first difference could be calculated based on the difference in shares between the values of the independent variables in the observed sam-ple (X_{iO}) and a counterfactual scenario under which the values of one of the independent variables were different (X_{iC}). These different sets of values for the independent variables produce different sets of predicted probabilities p_{ijO} and p_{ijC}, which in turn lead to different estimated shares S_{jO} and S_{jC}. The change in shares between the observed and counterfactual scenarios is then given by:

$$\Delta S_j(X_{iO} \rightarrow X_{iC}) = S_{jC} - S_{jO}, \tag{7}$$

where S_{jO} and S_{jC} are defined as in Equation 6.

I demonstrate the calculation of a first difference using changes in estimated population-level shares using the ITN example described above. In the sam-ple used to estimate the logit model presented in Table 1, approximately 64% of women reported exposure to a malaria-related educational message in the

---

[8] These predicted values are sometimes compared to the observed values of y to calculate the "percent correctly predicted" and related measures of goodness of fit (Herron 1999).

Table 4 Changes in predicted share using an ITN based on malaria education message

	Median	**(se)**	**95% CI**	
Current Message Exposure	76.402	(0.596)	75.224	77.597
Complete Message Exposure	77.542	(0.736)	76.140	78.992
Current → Complete	1.126	(0.425)	0.330	1.991

Note: Estimated shares were based on the logit model presented in Table 1, and are displayed as percentages. Standard errors and confidence intervals were calculated using 1000 sets of simulated coefficients.

six months before the survey. To estimate the substantive effect of these messages, I calculated the predicted share of women that used an ITN based on the observed values of the independent variables, and compared it to a counterfactual scenario under which all women were exposed to a malaria education message (this counterfactual scenario was created by simply setting the malaria education message dummy variable to 1 for all individuals in the sample). I multiplied the estimated shares by 100 in order to express them as percentages, and accounted for statistical uncertainty using the method of simulated coefficients with 1000 draws.

Applying sample enumeration with the appropriate sample weights to the observed data indicated that approximately 76.4% of women ages 15–49 used an ITN the previous night. Under the counterfactual scenario under which all women were exposed to a malaria education message, use of ITNs in this demographic group would have increased by approximately 1.1 percentage points. The 95% confidence interval on this increase does not overlap zero, indicating that it is statistically significant at the 5% level.

3.2 Marginal Effects and Elasticities

Another way to to estimate the substantive effect of an independent variable in a discrete choice model is to calculate the partial derivative of the choice probability curve with respect to the independent variable, holding the values of the other independent variables constant. This calculation yields the instantaneous rate of change of the probability curve at that point, which is equal to the slope of the tangent line to the probability curve at that value. This tangent line is a linear approximation of the probability curve at the selected point. This value could be interpreted as the effect of a 1-unit change in the independent variable on the choice probability, but this approximation is unlikely to be accurate if

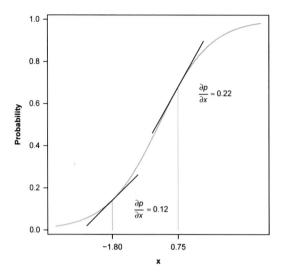

Figure 3 Marginal effects at different values of x

this represents a large change in the value of the independent variable. These calculations are known as *marginal effects* or *partial effects*. Figure 3 presents some examples of marginal effects for the logit probability curve presented in Figure 1, panel (a).

In binary choice models the marginal effect for an independent variable x_v is given by:[9]

$$\frac{\partial p}{\partial x_v} = \frac{\partial F(X\beta)}{\partial X\beta} \frac{\partial X\beta}{\partial x_v} = f(X\beta)\beta_v. \tag{8}$$

Note that if x_v is interacted with another variable, the marginal effect will also depend on the interaction term (Ai and Norton 2003; Greene and Hensher 2010; Norton, Wang, and Ai 2004).[10]

The marginal effects in a binary choice model are maximized when $X\beta = 0$. To see this, consider the marginal effects for a binary logit model:

$$\frac{\partial \Lambda(X\beta)}{\partial x_v} = \lambda(X\beta)\beta_v = \Lambda(X\beta)(1 - \Lambda(X\beta))\beta_v. \tag{9}$$

When $X\beta = 0$, the choice probability is equal to 0.5, and the largest marginal effect for x_v in a logit is $0.25 \times \beta_v$. This is sometimes known as the "divide by four" rule, since the largest possible marginal effect for a variable

---

[9] This calculation can be verified by calculating a first difference for a small change ϵ in x_v, and then dividing the result by ϵ to estimate the effect of a one-unit change in x_v.

[10] For example, if $X\beta = \beta_0 + \beta_1 x_1 + \beta_2 x_2 + \beta_{12}(x_1 x_2)$, then $\frac{\partial p}{\partial x_1} = f(X\beta)(\beta_1 + \beta_{12}x_2)$.

can be quickly calculated by dividing its coefficient by 4 (Gelman and Hill 2007, p. 82).[11]

Note that the partial derivative of the choice probability curve is only defined for a continuous x_v. Thus, marginal effects are typically regarded as an inappropriate measure of the substantive effect of dummy variables and other discontinuous variables – first differences rather than marginal effects should be used in most of these cases.

Since the relationship between the independent variables and the choice probabilities is nonlinear, the marginal effect of a variable x_v will depend both on the particular value of x_v and on the values of the other independent variables. As with first differences, marginal effects can be calculated for any set of values for X. However, there are two standard approaches. The first is to calculate the marginal effects at $\bar{X}$. This is known as the *marginal effect at the mean* (MEM), which for a logit is:

$$\text{MEM}(x_v) = \Lambda(\bar{X}\beta)(1 - \Lambda(\bar{X}\beta))\beta_v. \qquad (10)$$

The second approach is to calculate the marginal effects for each observation in the sample at its observed values, and then calculate the weighted mean of the marginal effects across observations. This is known as the *average partial effect* or the *average marginal effect* (AME), which for a logit is:

$$\text{AME}(x_v) = \frac{\sum_{i=1}^{n} \Lambda(X_i\beta)(1 - \Lambda(X_i\beta))\beta_v w_i}{\sum_{i=1}^{n} w_i}, \qquad (11)$$

where w_i are the sampling weights as described.

The MEM creates a hypothetical case with all independent variables set to their means, and reports the slope of the tangent line at the mean of x_v for that hypothetical case, while the AME calculates a tangent line for each observation in the sample at each observation's observed values, and then averages the tangent line slopes across the sample. Most researchers favor the AME, since $\bar{X}$ may represent a nonexistent or nonsensical hypothetical observation (for example, when X includes dummy variables). However, I will describe the MEM in all examples which follow, both for purposes of comparison with the AME and because the same approach used to calculate the MEM can be used to calculate the marginal effect for any hypothetical case of interest.

A common way to assess the relative influence of two different independent variables on the choice probabilities is to calculate the ratio of their marginal

---

[11] The largest marginal effect for x_v in a probit is $\frac{1}{2\pi}\beta_v \approx 0.4\beta_v$. Since logit coefficients are approximately 1.6 times larger than probit coefficients, multiplying logit coefficients by 0.25 and multiplying the equivalent probit coefficients by 0.4 will produce approximately equal marginal effects ($0.4 = 1.6 \times 0.25$).

effects. The ratio of the marginal effects for two variables x_v and x_z is simply the ratio of their coefficients:

$$\frac{\partial p}{\partial x_v} \Big/ \frac{\partial p}{\partial x_z} = \frac{f(X\beta)\beta_v}{f(X\beta)\beta_z} = \beta_v/\beta_z. \tag{12}$$

This ratio reveals the change in x_z that would be required in order to produce the same change in the choice probability as a 1-unit change in x_v. For example, if $\beta_v/\beta_z = 2$, then both a 1-unit increase in x_v and a 2-unit increase in x_z will produce the same change in $X\beta$, and thus the same change in the choice probability. Ratios of discrete choice coefficients are most commonly seen as *willingness to pay* (WTP) calculations, where β_z is a price or cost coefficient and β_v is a coefficient on some other attribute. In that case, the ratio β_v/β_z indicates the change in price that would be required to produce the same change in the choice probability as a 1-unit increase in x_v. Since the price coefficient β_z is usually negative, this ratio is usually multiplied by -1 and interpreted as the amount an individual would be willing to pay for one additional unit of x_v. Other applications are of course possible.

Marginal effects can also be presented as *elasticities*. The elasticity gives the percentage change in the choice probability that would result from a 1% increase in the independent variable of interest x_v – for instance, an elasticity of 2 indicates that a 1% increase in x_v leads to a 2% increase in the choice probability. Elasticities with an absolute value greater than 1 indicate an *elastic* relationship (a proportionately larger response in the choice probability for a given change in the independent variable), while elasticities with an absolute value less than 1 indicate an *inelastic* relationship (a proportionately smaller response in the choice probability for a given change in the independent variable).

In binary choice models the elasticity of the choice probability with respect to an independent variable x_v is calculated by dividing the changes in the probability and the independent variable by the values at which the elasticity is being calculated. This is equivalent to multiplying the marginal effect by x_v/p:[12]

$$\frac{\partial p/p}{\partial x_v/x_v} = \frac{\partial p}{\partial x_v} \frac{x_v}{p} = f(X\beta)\beta_v \frac{x_v}{p}. \tag{13}$$

The elasticity for a binary logit is thus:

$$\mathcal{E}(x_v) = \Lambda(X\beta)(1 - \Lambda(X\beta))\beta_v \frac{x_v}{\Lambda(X\beta)} = (1 - \Lambda(X\beta))x_v\beta_v. \tag{14}$$

---

[12] In some cases the formula for the elasticity is written as $\frac{\partial \ln p}{\partial \ln x_v}$. This is equivalent to Equation 13 as long as x_v is positive.

Table 5 Marginal effects and elasticities related to altitude of residence and ITN use

	Median	**(se)**	**95% CI**	
Average Marginal Effect (AME)	−0.063	(0.024)	−0.110	−0.017
Marginal Effect at the Mean (MEM)	−0.063	(0.025)	−0.116	−0.016
Average Elasticity	−0.105	(0.040)	−0.186	−0.029
Elasticity at the Mean	−0.102	(0.040)	−0.188	−0.026

Note: Estimates were based on the logit model presented in Table 1. Standard errors and confidence intervals were calculated using 1000 sets of simulated coefficients.

As with marginal effects, elasticities are often either calculated at the sample mean (elasticity at the mean), or calculated for all observations and then averaged (average elasticity).

Note that the elasticity in Equation 14 applies to a specific individual. Aggregate elasticities (the responsiveness of a group of individuals to an incremental change in x_v) are calculated as the weighted average of the individual elasticities in the sample, using the choice probabilities (and sample weights) as weights (Ben-Akiva and Lerman 1985, pp. 112–113; Hensher, Rose, and Greene 2015, pp. 373–374; Louviere, Hensher, and Swait 2000, p. 60). This approach to calculating aggregate elasticities is sometimes known as *probability weighted sample enumeration*. Also note that the elasticity in Equation 14 is a *point elasticity*, because it is calculated at a single point on the probability curve. It is also possible to calculate an *arc elasticity*, which measures the elasticity between two different points on the probability curve. An arc elasticity can be determined from a first difference by calculating the percentage change in the choice probability divided by the percentage change in the independent variable of interest. In this Element I will focus on individual-level point elasticities.

Table 5 presents the marginal effects and elasticities of altitude of residence in the ITN use example. Uncertainty in these substantive effects was estimated using the method of simulated coefficients with 1000 draws.

The AME gives the average marginal effect across all individuals in the sample, while the MEM gives the marginal effect calculated at the sample mean. In this case both approaches produced nearly identical marginal effects, although in other cases the AME and MEM can diverge significantly. The marginal effect was negative and statistically significant, as expected from the negative coefficient on altitude of residence in Table 1. These marginal effects could be interpreted as the effect of a 1-unit increase in altitude of residence (1000 meters) on the probability of using an ITN, but, as discussed, this approximation is unlikely to be accurate for such a large change in the independent variable. Instead, these marginal effects are best described as the slope of the line that gives the change in probability for a very small increase in altitude of residence.

The average elasticity across the sample and the elasticity at the mean are based on the AME and the MEM, respectively, and so were also quite similar in this example. These elasticities indicate that for a 1% increase in altitude of residence, the probability of sleeping under an ITN decreased by slightly more than −0.1%. Thus, the probability of ITN use is relatively inelastic with respect to altitude of residence, with a given increase in altitude of residence producing a proportionately smaller decrease in the probability of sleeping under an ITN. As with marginal effects, elasticities are best interpreted as the expected effect from a very small increase in altitude of residence.

The relative influence of two different variables on the decision to sleep under an ITN can be calculated as the ratio of the coefficients on those variables. For instance, I calculated the relative influence of exposure to a malaria education message on the decision to sleep under an ITN in terms of altitude of residence as the coefficient on exposure to a malaria education message divided by the coefficient on altitude of residence. This yields the influence of exposure to a malaria education message in terms of thousands of meters of altitude of residence. Uncertainty in this substantive effect was estimated using the method of simulated coefficients with 1000 draws (calculating and summarizing 1000 ratios of coefficients). The median ratio across the 1000 sets of simulated coefficients was −0.513 (95% CI: −1.752, −0.101). Thus, if a woman was exposed to a malaria education message in the last six months, she was expected to change her ITN use in the same way as if she had moved to a new residence 513 meters lower in altitude, where malaria is more common.

3.3 Odds Ratios

A third way to calculate substantive effects in discrete choice models is through *odds ratios*. In a binary choice model, the odds of observing $y = 1$ are given by $p/(1 - p)$, which measures the number of observations where $y = 1$ for every observation where $y = 0$. The odds ratio is simply the ratio of the odds under two different sets of values of the independent variables X_A and X_B. If p_A is the probability of observing $y = 1$ with X_A, and p_B is the probability of observing $y = 1$ with X_B, then the odds ratio that results from changing from from X_A to X_B is given by $(p_B/(1 - p_B))/(p_A/(1 - p_A))$.[13] An odds ratio greater than 1

---

[13] Odds ratios are sometimes mistaken for *risk ratios*. The risk ratio (also known as the *relative risk*) in this case is p_B/p_A. Odds ratios and risk ratios will often be quite different, although if

indicates that changing from X_A to X_B increases the expected odds of observing $y = 1$, while an odds ratio less than 1 indicates the opposite.

While it is possible to calculate odds ratios for a probit model, the properties of the exponential function leads to very simple calculations of odds ratios in logit models. The odds of observing $y = 1$ in the binary logit model are given by:

$$\frac{p}{(1-p)} = \frac{\exp(X\beta)/(1 + \exp(X\beta))}{1/(1 + \exp(X\beta))} = \exp(X\beta). \tag{15}$$

Following from the properties of the exponential function, for any independent variable x_v, the odds can be rewritten as:

$$\exp(X\beta) = \exp(X_{-v}\beta_{-v})\exp(x_v\beta_v), \tag{16}$$

where $X_{-v}\beta_{-v}$ is the linear function of independent variables and coefficients omitting $x_v\beta_v$. If x_v is increased by 1 unit, the odds then become:

$$\exp(X_{-v}\beta_{-v})\exp((x_v + 1)\beta_v) = \exp(X_{-v}\beta_{-v})\exp(x_v\beta_v)\exp(\beta_v)$$
$$= \exp(X\beta)\exp(\beta_v). \tag{17}$$

That is, if an independent variable x_v increases by 1 unit, it produces a multiplicative change in the odds of observing $y = 1$ of $\exp(\beta_v)$. If X_B is identical to X_A, except that x_v has been increased by 1 unit, then the odds ratio when changing from X_A to X_B is:

$$OR(X_A \rightarrow X_B) = \exp(X_B\beta)/\exp(X_A\beta)$$
$$= \exp(X\beta)\exp(\beta_v)/\exp(X\beta) = \exp(\beta_v). \tag{18}$$

Thus, to calculate an odds ratio in a binary logit model, simply multiply the relevant coefficient by whatever change in the independent variable is of interest, and then exponentiate. The change in the odds of observing $y = 1$ for a δ-unit change in x_v is $\exp(\beta_v\delta)$. The percentage change in odds for a δ-unit change in x_v can be calculated as $100 \times (\exp(\beta_v\delta) - 1)$.

The odds of observing $y = 0$ are simply the inverse of the odds of observing $y = 1$, and thus the odds ratios for $y = 0$ for a δ-unit change in x_v are given by the inverse of the odds ratio for $y = 1$ for the same δ-unit change in x_v, or $1/\exp(\beta_v\delta) = \exp(-\beta_v\delta)$.

---

p_A and p_B are low, the odds ratio and the risk ratio should be approximately equal – this is often known as the *rare disease assumption* (Manski 1995, pp. 75–78).

Unlike the other substantive effects discussed here, the odds ratio usually does not depend on the values of X.[14] A 1-unit change in x_v will lead to a constant factor change in the odds, regardless of the values of the other independent variables or the starting value of x_v.[15] This, plus the simplicity of the calculation in logit models, are attractive features of the odds ratio.

While the odds ratio for a 1-unit change in an independent variable is given by the exponentiated coefficient, simply exponentiating the standard error on that coefficient is not an appropriate measure of uncertainty (since standard errors are always positive, exponentiating will always generate values of at least 1). The delta method is often used to calculate the standard error of odds ratios. The derivative of $\exp(\beta)$ is simply $\exp(\beta)$, so by Equation 1, $se(OR) = \sqrt{(\exp(\beta))^2 \mathrm{Var}(\beta)} = \exp(\beta)se(\beta)$. However, since odds ratios are bounded below at 0, but have no upper bound, the sampling distribution of the odds ratio is likely to be non-normal in practical application, reducing the accuracy of the delta method. Confidence intervals constructed using standard errors calculated with the delta method might also include negative odds ratios. Confidence intervals on odds ratios can instead be calculated by exponentiating the endpoints of the equivalent confidence interval on β (e.g., Agresti 2013; Mandel 2013). Another approach to calculating standard errors and confidence intervals is to generate a set of coefficients through simulation or bootstrapping, exponentiate them, and then summarize them appropriately.

Table 6 presents the odds ratios from the ITN use example associated with a 1-unit change in each independent variable. Median odds ratios, standard errors and 95% confidence intervals were calculated using the method of simulated coefficients.

Recall that odds ratios produce a multiplicative change in the odds. For example, exposure to a malaria-related educational message changes the odds of ITN use by a factor of 1.2 (an increase of approximately 20%), while a 1-unit (1000 meter) increase in altitude of residence changes the odds of ITN use by a factor of 0.7 (a decrease of approximately 30%).

---

[14] However, this is not true if the variable of interest is interacted with another variable, since the change in the odds will also depend on the interaction term (Norton, Wang, and Ai 2004). For example, if $X\beta = \beta_0 + \beta_1 x_1 + \beta_2 x_2 + \beta_{12}(x_1 x_2)$, then the odds ratio resulting from a 1-unit change in x_1 is $\exp(\beta_1 + \beta_{12} x_2)$.

[15] Note that a constant factor change in the odds is not the same as a constant factor change in p. For example, an odds ratio of 2 shifts odds of $1/1$ to $2/1$, which changes p from 0.5 to 0.667 (an increase of 0.167). However, this same odds ratio shifts odds of $2/1$ to $4/1$, which changes p from 0.667 to 0.8 (an increase of 0.133).

Table 6 Odds ratios in the logit model for use of an ITN

Independent Variable	Median	(se)	95% CI	
Malaria Education Message	1.205	(0.085)	1.046	1.373
Years of Education	0.968	(0.009)	0.951	0.987
Top Wealth Quartile	0.789	(0.069)	0.665	0.935
Bottom Wealth Quartile	1.095	(0.097)	0.909	1.294
Pregnant	1.038	(0.127)	0.810	1.324
Altitude of Residence	0.701	(0.093)	0.532	0.912
Number of Observations	5,119			

Note: Estimates were based on the logit model presented in Table 1. Median odds ratios, standard errors and confidence intervals were calculated using 1000 sets of simulated coefficients.

4 Substantive Effects in Ordered Choice Models

I now extend the techniques for interpreting binary choice models to choice situations with more than two categories. Here I consider models for choices from a set of categories that are ordered in some way. The example presented in this section is an examination of individual-level forecasts for household finances over the next year ranging from "much worse" to "much better." There are dozens of other examples, most commonly from survey instruments that ask respondents to rate an item on an ordered scale.

Ordered choice models assume the J categories of the dependent variable y_i are ordered, with 1 representing the lowest category and J representing the highest. The choice probabilities p_{ij} are a function of observed independent variables and estimated coefficients $X_i\beta$ such that larger values of $X_i\beta$ increase the probability of choosing higher categories. The probability that individual i chooses category j in this model is specified as:

$$p_{ij} = \Pr(y_i = j|X_i) = F(\tau_j - X_i\beta) - F(\tau_{j-1} - X_i\beta), \tag{19}$$

where τ_j is the "threshold" (constant term) for the binary choice model $F(\tau_j - X_i\beta)$ for the choice between category j or lower and category $j + 1$ or higher, $\tau_0 = -\infty$ (so that the probability of choosing the lowest category is $F(\tau_1 - X_i\beta)$) and $\tau_J = +\infty$ (so that the probability of choosing the highest category is $1 - F(\tau_{J-1} - X_i\beta)$).[16]

---

[16] The term "threshold" comes from a latent variable motivation for ordered choice models, in which the observed choice is based on the value of an underlying latent variable relative to a set of $J - 1$ thresholds that divide the latent variable into J choice categories.

Different ordered choice models are defined by the choice of the CDF $F(.)$. Setting $F(.)$ to the cumulative standard logistic distribution leads to the *ordered logit* model, while setting $F(.)$ to the cumulative standard normal distribution leads to the *ordered probit* model. This section will focus on the ordered logit, but all of the techniques presented here apply equally to the ordered probit except where noted.

4.1 Example: Anticipated Election Outcomes and Forecasts of Household Economic Well-Being in the US

Do voters believe that an election victory by their preferred US presidential candidate will improve their household's economic well-being? A large number of studies have examined the relationship between economic perceptions and voting behavior in the United States, and generally agree that voters rely on evaluations of the state of the national economy ("sociotropic" evaluations) rather than personal economic considerations ("pocketbook" or "egocentric" evaluations) when casting a vote (e.g., Kiewiet 1983; Kinder and Kiewiet 1981; Lewis-Beck 1988; Lewis-Beck and Paldam 2000). However, sociotropic voters may still link election outcomes to their own personal financial situation, or even be motivated by economic self-interest, viewing the state of the national economy as the best indication of whether the incumbent will produce economic conditions that benefit them personally.

Here I examine the relationship between anticipated election outcomes and forecasts of household economic well-being. The data in this example consist of 731 face-to-face interviews conducted during the pre-election wave of the 2016 American National Election Study (The American National Election Studies (ANES) 2019). One survey question asked respondents:

> Now looking ahead, do you think that a year from now [you / you and your family living here] will be much better off financially, somewhat better off, about the same, somewhat worse off, or much worse off than now?

The dependent variable y_i is coded as five ordered categories ("Much Worse," "Somewhat Worse," "Same," "Somewhat Better," and "Much Better"), with higher numbers indicating greater optimism.

I modeled these household financial forecasts as a function of several independent variables. The key independent variable in this example was a dummy variable indicating whether the respondent anticipated that their preferred presidential candidate would win the election (1 = preferred candidate will win, 0 otherwise). This variable was based on both the respondent's stated vote intention and their prediction for the outcome of the US presidential election.[17] If respondents were linking their household economic situation to the outcome of the election, then respondents who believed their preferred presidential candidate would win should have been more optimistic about their household's financial future.

Respondents were also asked to rate their personal health on a five-point scale, with higher numbers indicating better health.[18] Worse health was expected to lead to more pessimistic forecasts for future household finances, as respondents grapple with medical costs and a reduced ability to work. Respondents who were paying off a mortgage on their home (1 = paying off mortgage, 0 = otherwise) were also expected to be more pessimistic about future household finances, as many recent home buyers had stretched their finances to afford a home. The model also included gender (1 = female, 0 = male) and age (measured in years). Women were expected to be more pessimistic about their future household finances due to reduced earning power relative to men, while older respondents were expected to be more pessimistic due to the end of their earning years and the anticipation of future medical costs. Table 7 presents the results of estimating an ordered logit model on these data.

The interpretation of the coefficients in an ordered choice model is similar to the interpretation of the coefficients in a binary choice model. Positive coefficients indicate that as the value of the independent variable increases, the probability of observing a response in the higher categories of the ordered dependent variable increases, while the probability of observing responses in the lower categories decreases (negative coefficients of course have the opposite effect). The results in Table 7 demonstrate that respondents who predicted a favorable election outcome and who rated their personal health more highly were more likely to have optimistic expectations for their future household finances. Conversely, having a mortgage and increasing age tended to produce more pessimistic expectations, while gender did not have a statistically significant effect at the 5% level. Four "threshold" constant terms are presented, one for each pair of adjacent choice categories. For instance, "Threshold MW/SW" indicates the threshold between the categories "much worse" and "somewhat worse," which is the constant term in the binary logit model with "much worse" and "somewhat worse" or higher as the choice categories. These constant terms

---

[17] Seven respondents who predicted a win for a third party candidate were omitted from the analysis.

[18] The categories on the health self-assessment scale were "poor," "fair," "good," "very good," and "excellent."

Table 7 Ordered logit model for predicted household finances in one year

Independent Variable	Coefficient	(se)	95% CI	
Predicts Favorable Election Outcome	0.651	(0.185)	0.289	1.013
Self-Rating of Personal Health	0.239	(0.068)	0.106	0.373
Paying Off Mortgage	−0.352	(0.142)	−0.630	−0.074
Female	−0.048	(0.140)	−0.321	0.226
Age	−0.021	(0.004)	−0.029	−0.013
Threshold MW/SW	−4.235	(0.470)	−5.156	−3.313
Threshold SW/S	−2.081	(0.380)	−2.826	−1.335
Threshold S/SB	0.492	(0.371)	−0.234	1.218
Threshold SB/MB	2.133	(0.379)	1.391	2.876
Number of Observations	731			

Note: Dependent variable categories are "Much Worse" (MW), "Somewhat Worse" (SW), "Same" (S), "Somewhat Better" (SB), and "Much Better" (MB).

are typically regarded as nuisance parameters (similar to the constant term in a binary choice model), and are not usually interpreted in a substantive way.

4.2 First Differences

For two different sets of values for the independent variables (X_A and X_B), the first difference for choice category j in an ordered choice model is calculated as:

$$\Delta p_j(X_A \rightarrow X_B) = \Pr(y_i = j|X_B) - \Pr(y_i = j|X_A), \tag{20}$$

where the choice probability $\Pr(y_i = j|X)$ is defined as in Equation 19. Except for the lowest and highest categories of the dependent variable, the first differences for a change in x_v for a choice category may be positive or negative, regardless of the sign of β_v.

I calculated the substantive effect of individual election forecasts on predicted household finances through a first difference. I began by creating two different hypothetical cases, one with an optimistic forecast for the presidential election (preferred candidate wins), and the other with a pessimistic forecast (preferred candidate loses). All other variables were held constant at their medians across both hypothetical cases.[19] I then calculated predicted

---

[19] This hypothetical individual was female, 52 years old, did not have a mortgage, and rated her health as "good."

Table 8 First differences in predicted household finances based on predictions for a favorable election outcome

	Median	**(se)**	**95% CI**	
Much Worse				
Optimistic	0.012	(0.004)	0.006	0.021
Pessimistic	0.022	(0.008)	0.011	0.042
Optimistic → Pessimistic	0.010	(0.005)	0.003	0.023
Somewhat Worse				
Optimistic	0.079	(0.012)	0.059	0.105
Pessimistic	0.140	(0.025)	0.099	0.192
Optimistic → Pessimistic	0.061	(0.021)	0.023	0.104
The Same				
Optimistic	0.473	(0.023)	0.427	0.519
Pessimistic	0.551	(0.023)	0.502	0.595
Optimistic → Pessimistic	0.076	(0.021)	0.037	0.117
Somewhat Better				
Optimistic	0.305	(0.021)	0.266	0.348
Pessimistic	0.212	(0.028)	0.163	0.269
Optimistic → Pessimistic	−0.092	(0.026)	−0.141	−0.040
Much Better				
Optimistic	0.129	(0.017)	0.099	0.166
Pessimistic	0.071	(0.014)	0.048	0.105
Optimistic → Pessimistic	−0.058	(0.016)	−0.087	−0.027

Note: Estimates were based on the ordered logit model presented in Table 7. Standard errors and confidence intervals were calculated using 1000 sets of simulated coefficients.

probabilities for each of the five choice categories for both hypothetical cases, with uncertainty in these probabilities calculated using the method of simulated coefficients with 1000 draws. The first difference was then calculated as the difference between the predicted probabilities for each choice category. Table 8 presents the results from the predicted probability and first difference calculations across the 1000 simulated coefficients.

As expected, when the election forecast for this hypothetical case changed from optimistic to pessimistic, the probability of forecasting a "much better" or "somewhat better" household financial situation decreased, while the probability of forecasting a "much worse," "somewhat worse," or "the same" household financial situation increased. None of the 95% confidence intervals on these

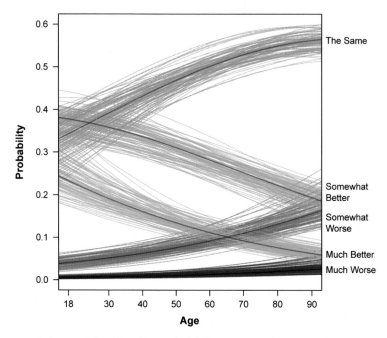

Figure 4 Predicted household finances as a function of age

changes overlap zero, demonstrating that these differences are statistically significant at the 5% level.

Another example of first difference calculations is demonstrated in Figure 4, which presents the changes in the predicted probabilities from the ordered logit model in Table 7 as age varies, holding all other independent variables at their median values.[20] Uncertainty in these probabilities was calculated using the method of simulated coefficients with 1000 draws. All 1000 predicted probability curves generated from the 1000 sets of simulated coefficients are presented for each choice category, with the probability curves for the mean of the draws presented as a darker line.

The coefficient on age is negative, so the probability for the most optimistic category of the dependent variable ("much better") declines as age increases, while the probability of the most pessimistic category ("much worse") increases as age increases. For the intermediate choice categories, the choice probabilities are not guaranteed to be uniformly increasing or decreasing as an independent variable increases, although no reversals in sign for these choice categories are apparent in this particular case.

---

[20] The hypothetical case examined here is a female who did not have a mortgage, rated her health as "good," and predicted that her favored presidential candidate would win the election.

The substantive effects of the independent variable can also be summarized across the choice categories – for instance, by calculating the mean of the absolute value of the first differences across all choice categories (Long 1997, p. 137).

4.3 Marginal Effects and Elasticities

Each of the J choice categories in an ordered choice model will have a separate marginal effect or elasticity, which gives the slope of the tangent line to each of the J probability curves at some given values of X.

In ordered choice models the marginal effect of an independent variable x_v for choice category j is given by:

$$\frac{\partial p_j}{\partial x_v} = \frac{\partial F(\tau_j - X\beta)}{\partial x_v} - \frac{\partial F(\tau_{j-1} - X\beta)}{\partial x_v}$$
$$= [f(\tau_j - X\beta) - \beta_v] - [f(\tau_{j-1} - X\beta) - \beta_v]$$
$$= [f(\tau_{j-1} - X\beta) - f(\tau_j - X\beta)]\beta_v \tag{21}$$

where F and f are the CDF and PDF of the appropriate distribution (e.g., logistic for ordered logit). As with binary choice models, the marginal effect of a variable x_v will depend both on the particular value of x_v and on the values of the other independent variables. Marginal effects are frequently reported as the weighted average of the marginal effects across all individuals in the sample (the AME), or the marginal effect calculated at the sample mean (the MEM).

The marginal effects in ordered choice models will sum to zero across all choice categories. The marginal effects in ordered choice models also have the *single crossing property* (Greene and Hensher 2010), which means the marginal effects will change sign exactly once across the sequence of choice categories from 1 to J.

As with the binary choice models, the relative influence of two different independent variables on the choice probabilities can be determined through the ratio of their marginal effects:

$$\frac{\partial p}{\partial x_v} / \frac{\partial p}{\partial x_z} = [f(\tau_j - X\beta) - f(\tau_{j-1} - X\beta)]\beta_v / [f(\tau_j - X\beta) - f(\tau_{j-1} - X\beta)]\beta_z$$
$$= \beta_v / \beta_z. \tag{22}$$

In the case of ordered choice models, this ratio reveals the change in x_z that would be required in order to produce the same change in the choice probabilities across all categories as a 1-unit change in x_v.

The elasticity of the choice probability for choice category j with respect to an independent variable x_v is given by:

$$\frac{\partial p_j / p_j}{\partial x_v / x_v} = \frac{\partial p_j}{\partial x_v} \frac{x_v}{p_j} = [f(\tau_{j-1} - X\beta) - f(\tau_j - X\beta)]\beta_v \frac{x_v}{p_j}. \tag{23}$$

These elasticities are frequently calculated as the weighted average across all observations (average elasticity), or calculated at the sample mean (elasticity at the mean).

Table 9 presents the marginal effects and elasticities related to self-rating of personal health in the predicted household finances example.[21] Since self-rated health had a positive coefficient and by the single crossing property, all of these estimated substantive effects will be negative for the lowest choice category and positive for the highest choice category, with one sign switch as the choice categories increase. Uncertainty on these substantive effects was estimated using the method of simulated coefficients with 1000 draws.

The AME and the MEM for each choice category are very similar in value, as are the average elasticity and the elasticity at the mean. All of these substantive effects switch from negative to positive at the same point as the choice categories increase, as expected from the single crossing property. Overall, these results indicate a somewhat inelastic relationship between self-rated health and predicted household finances. For example, the average elasticity indicates that a 1% increase in the self-rated health scale reduces the probability of selecting a forecast of "much worse" by about 0.8%.

The relative influence of two different independent variables on the choice probabilities is calculated as the ratio of the coefficients on those variables. For instance, I calculated the relative effect of paying off a mortgage in terms of age as the ratio of the coefficients on these variables, accounting for uncertainty by using the method of simulated coefficients with 1000 draws. The median ratio across the 1000 sets of simulated coefficients is 16.991 (95% CI: 3.358, 33.941), indicating that if a voter was paying a mortgage, this had the same effect on household economic forecasts across all five choice categories as if the voter became 17 years older.

4.4 Odds Ratios

Odds ratios for ordered choice models can be calculated for any two groupings of categories of the dependent variable, but the odds that are most typically considered are the odds of observing a choice in categories 1 through j versus

---

[21] For this example, I assumed the self-rating of personal health could be treated as a continuous variable.

Table 9 Marginal effects and elasticities related to self-reported health and predicted household finances

	Median	**(se)**	**95% CI**	
Much Worse				
AME	−0.003	(0.002)	−0.007	−0.001
MEM	−0.003	(0.001)	−0.006	−0.001
Average Elasticity	−0.835	(0.240)	−1.289	−0.348
Elasticity at the Mean	−0.823	(0.236)	−1.271	−0.343
Somewhat Worse				
AME	−0.019	(0.006)	−0.031	−0.008
MEM	−0.019	(0.006)	−0.030	−0.009
Average Elasticity	−0.750	(0.217)	−1.163	−0.308
Elasticity at the Mean	−0.738	(0.213)	−1.139	−0.303
The Same				
AME	−0.031	(0.009)	−0.048	−0.013
MEM	−0.036	(0.011)	−0.058	−0.015
Average Elasticity	−0.290	(0.092)	−0.478	−0.116
Elasticity at the Mean	−0.246	(0.075)	−0.399	−0.102
Somewhat Better				
AME	0.027	(0.008)	0.012	0.042
MEM	0.033	(0.010)	0.014	0.054
Average Elasticity	0.341	(0.095)	0.152	0.521
Elasticity at the Mean	0.398	(0.119)	0.167	0.628
Much Better				
AME	0.027	(0.008)	0.011	0.043
MEM	0.025	(0.007)	0.010	0.038
Average Elasticity	0.721	(0.205)	0.304	1.108
Elasticity at the Mean	0.737	(0.213)	0.306	1.142

Note: Estimates were based on the ordered logit model presented in Table 7. Standard errors and confidence intervals were calculated using 1000 sets of simulated coefficients.

a choice in categories $j + 1$ through J (or equivalently, the odds of observing a choice below versus above a choice threshold τ_j).

   Recall from the description of Equation 19 that the binary choice model $F(\tau_j − X\beta)$ gives the probability of observing a choice of category j or lower. Thus, the odds ratio for a choice below versus above a choice threshold τ_j in an ordered choice model can be derived in the same way as for a binary choice model. As with the binary logit model, the properties of the exponential function lead to very simple calculations of odds ratios in ordered logit models. Odds ratios are almost never used in interpreting ordered probit models, although it is possible to do.

Inserting $\tau_j - X\beta$ in place of $X\beta$ in Equation 15 shows that the odds of observing $y \leq j$ in an ordered logit model are given by $\exp(\tau_j - X\beta)$. Then following Equation 18, if an independent variable x_v increases by 1 unit, it produces a multiplicative change in the odds of observing $y \leq j$ of $\exp(-\beta_v)$. Just as in a binary choice model, a 1-unit change in x_v in an ordered choice model will lead to a constant factor change in the odds, regardless of the values of the other independent variables or the starting value of x_v. Most importantly, the odds ratios in ordered choice models do not depend on the value of the threshold τ_j, which means that the multiplicative change in the odds of observing $y \leq j$ will be the same for any choice category j. This property of ordered choice models is known as the *proportional odds* or *parallel regression* assumption.[22]

The odds of observing $y > j$ are simply the inverse of the odds of observing $y \leq j$, and thus the change in the odds of observing $y > j$ for a δ-unit change in x_v is given by the inverse of the change in the odds of observing $y \leq j$ for the same δ-unit change in x_v, or $1/\exp(-\beta_k\delta) = \exp(\beta_k\delta)$. Thus, just as in a binary logit model, the odds ratio associated with being over a choice threshold in an ordered logit model can be calculated by simply multiplying the coefficients by whatever changes in the independent variables are of interest, and then exponentiating.

Table 10 presents the odds ratios for being over a choice threshold (more optimistic) versus below that threshold (more pessimistic) associated with a 1-unit change in each independent variable. Median odds ratios, standard errors and 95% confidence intervals were calculated using the method of simulated coefficients.

These odds ratios indicate that the odds of a more optimistic household economic forecast nearly doubled for those individuals who predicted a favorable election outcome as compared to those who did not. That is, predicting a favorable election outcome nearly doubled the odds that an individual will predict his or her household finances will be "much better" in the coming year versus the lower categories, nearly doubled the odds of predicting "much better" or "somewhat better" versus the lower categories, and so on.

---

[22] The term "parallel regression" comes from the observation that the probability of observing $y \leq j$ across the values of x_v is identical across choice categories, except that the curve for each choice category is shifted by the constant term τ_j (see Figure 1(b)). The proportional odds/parallel regression assumption applies to both ordered logit and ordered probit models.

Table 10 Odds ratios in the ordered logit model for predicted household finances

Independent Variable	Median	(se)	95% CI	
Predicts Favorable Election Outcome	1.893	(0.362)	1.312	2.673
Self-Rating of Personal Health	1.269	(0.087)	1.122	1.456
Paying Off Mortgage	0.714	(0.102)	0.534	0.940
Female	0.943	(0.131)	0.736	1.233
Age	0.979	(0.004)	0.972	0.987
Number of Observations	731			

Note: Dependent variable categories are "Much Worse" (MW), "Somewhat Worse" (SW), "Same" (S), "Somewhat Better" (SB), and "Much Better" (MB). Estimates were based on the ordered logit model presented in Table 7. Median odds ratios, standard errors and confidence intervals were calculated using 1000 sets of simulated coefficients.

5 Substantive Effects in Multinomial Choice Models

I now turn to models for choices from an unordered set of categories. The example presented in this section is an examination of vote choice in the 2015 British General Election. There are numerous other examples, such as choosing a mode of transportation (e.g., train, bus, or car) or choosing a geographic location to visit for recreation.

Multinomial choice models assume the J categories of the dependent variable are unordered. The choice probabilities p_{ij} are a function of observed independent variables and estimated coefficients. The independent variables can be *alternative invariant* (variables that vary across individuals but not choice alternatives, such as age), or *alternative specific* (variables that vary across both individuals and choice alternatives, such as the travel time from an individual's home to a recreation site).

This section will focus on the *multinomial logit (MNL)* model. Some researchers make a distinction between "multinomial logits" that only include alternative invariant variables, and *conditional logit (CL)* models, which also include alternative specific variables. Some researchers also refer to multinomial logit models that include both alternative invariant and alternative specific variables as "mixed logits." To avoid confusion with other statistical models that share these names I will always refer to the choice model discussed here as a multinomial logit, regardless of the type of independent variables included in the model.[23]

---

[23] There is also a *multinomial probit (MNP)* model, but estimation of this model is much more cumbersome, and it has generally been replaced in applied empirical work with the *mixed logit*

In the multinomial logit model, the probability that individual i chooses category j is specified as:

$$p_{ij} = \Pr(y_i = j | X_{ik}, A_i) = \frac{\exp(X_{ij}\beta + A_i\gamma_j)}{\sum_{k=1}^{J} \exp(X_{ik}\beta + A_i\gamma_k)}, \tag{24}$$

where X_{ik} are the alternative specific variables and A_i are the alternative invariant variables. The coefficients on the alternative invariant variables γ are subscripted by choice category, allowing those variables to have differing effects across choice categories – for instance, increasing age might increase the probability of selecting one choice category, and decrease the probability of selecting another. These coefficients are known as *alternative specific* coefficients. An identification constraint is necessary in order to estimate the alternative specific coefficients – the standard approach is to set $\gamma = 0$ for a "baseline" or "reference" category. With this constraint γ_j gives the effect of the alternative invariant variables on the choice of category j relative to the baseline category. No such identification constraint is necessary for the alternative specific variables. The coefficients on these variables are known as *generic* coefficients.

5.1 Example: Vote Choice in the 2015 British General Election

One of the most notable outcomes of the 2015 British General Election was the surge in the popularity of the United Kingdom Independence Party (UKIP), which replaced the Liberal Democrats as the third largest party by vote share in the United Kingdom (Hawkins, Keen, and Nakatudde 2015). The rise of the UKIP foreshadowed the "Brexit" referendum vote of 2016 – unlike the other major parties in the General Election, the UKIP openly advocated leaving the European Union (United Kingdom Independence Party 2015).

Here I consider the factors that influenced vote choice among the four largest political parties (in terms of vote share) that contested seats throughout Great Britain (England, Scotland, and Wales). For simplicity, I omit Northern Ireland (which has a different party system than Great Britain), regional parties that only contested seats in Scotland or Wales, and smaller parties such as the Green Party and dozens of minor parties. Going into the 2015 General Election the government was comprised of a coalition between the Conservative and Liberal Democrat parties. The Conservative Party did well in the 2015 election, remaining the largest party by vote share, and winning an outright majority of seats. In contrast, the Liberal Democrats collapsed in the 2015 election, losing 49 of their 57 seats. The UKIP supplanted the Liberal Democrats

---

model described in Section 6.2. The techniques discussed in this Element can also be extended to the MNP.

as the third largest party by vote share.[24] The opposition Labour Party gained vote share but lost seats, remaining the second largest party in the UK by both measures.

The data in this example come from the post-election wave of the 2015 British Election Study (Fieldhouse et al. 2016), which contained 890 face-to-face interviews conducted throughout Great Britain between May 8 (the day after the general election) and September 13, 2015. Each of these survey respondents voted for one of the four parties described here (respondents who voted for a party other than these four were omitted from the analysis). The dependent variable is each survey respondent's vote choice from among these four parties.[25]

The survey question most relevant to the rise of the UKIP asked respondents to rate their approval of British membership in the European Union (EU) on a five-point scale, with higher numbers indicating greater approval.[26] Voters with greater approval of EU membership were expected to be less likely to vote for the UKIP.

Several other individual voter characteristics were also included in the model. Respondents were asked to rate changes in the National Health Service (NHS) since the 2010 General Election on a five-point scale, with higher numbers indicating more positive opinions.[27] Voters with positive opinions of the NHS were expected to be more likely to prefer the incumbent Conservative and Liberal Democrat parties. The model also included income (measured on a 15-point scale, with higher numbers indicating higher income), gender (1 = female, 0 = male) and age (measured in years).

All of these independent variables are alternative invariant. The alternative specific coefficients for all of these variables are specified with the UKIP as the baseline category. I also included a constant term for each party except for the baseline party – these constant terms are known as *alternative specific constants*. These alternative specific constants are necessary in order for the

---

[24] Elections to the House of Commons use a "first past the post" system – in each of the 650 Parliamentary constituencies the candidate with the most votes is elected. Despite a vote share of 12.6%, the UKIP only won one seat due to its distribution of votes across constituencies. The Scottish National Party (SNP) was actually the third largest party in terms of seats after the 2015 election despite having a vote share of only 4.7%, due to its concentrated support in Scottish constituencies.

[25] Note that the UKIP did not contest 8 of the 272 Parliamentary constituencies represented in these data; survey respondents from these constituencies were omitted from the data.

[26] The categories on this approval scale were "strongly disapprove," "disapprove," "neither approve nor disapprove," "approve," and "strongly approve."

[27] The categories on this rating scale were "got a lot worse," "got a little worse," "stayed the same," "got a little better," and "got a lot better."

estimated choice probabilities to match the choice probabilities in the data, and are typically regarded as nuisance parameters not to be interpreted in a substantive way.

Survey respondents were also presented with a diagram of a 0 to 10 scale, with the low end of the scale labeled "government should cut taxes a lot and spend much less on health and social services," and the high end of the scale labeled "government should raise taxes a lot and spend much more on health and social services." Respondents were asked to rate their own preferences and their perceptions of each party's policies on this scale. The difference between each voter's self-placement and their placement of each party was included as an alternative specific independent variable with a generic coefficient. Voters were expected to prefer parties that were closer to their ideal position on this tax/spend scale to parties that were further from this ideal point. Table 11 presents the results of estimating a multinomial logit model on these data.

The interpretation of the alternative specific coefficients in a multinomial logit is straightforward, and similar to the interpretation of the coefficients in a binary choice model. Positive alternative specific coefficients indicate that as the value of the independent variable increases, the probability of selecting the choice category to which the coefficient applies increases, while the probability of selecting the baseline category decreases. Negative alternative specific coefficients of course have the opposite effect – increases in the values of these independent variables will decrease the probability of selecting the choice category to which the coefficient applies, and increase the probability of selecting the baseline category.

As expected, the results in Table 11 indicate that higher levels of approval of EU membership increased the probability of voting for the other major parties in the election relative to the UKIP (decreased the probability of voting for the UKIP relative to the other major parties).

More positive opinions of the NHS and higher income increased the probability of voting for the incumbent Conservative Party relative to the UKIP, but these variables were not statistically significant at the 5% level for the Labour/UKIP and Liberal Democrat/UKIP comparisons. Relative to the UKIP, women were more likely to vote for one of the other major parties, and older voters were more likely to vote Conservative and less likely to vote Labour.

As the value of an alternative invariant variable increases, the choice probability for the category with the largest alternative specific coefficient for that variable will uniformly increase, while the choice probability for the category with the smallest alternative specific coefficient will uniformly decrease. For

Table 11 Multinomial logit model for vote choice in the 2015 British General Election

Independent Variable	Coefficient	(se)	95% CI	
Difference on Tax/Spend	−0.393	(0.032)	−0.456	−0.331
Approves of Britain in EU:				
Conservative	0.743	(0.111)	0.526	0.960
Labour	0.986	(0.117)	0.756	1.215
Liberal Democrat	1.059	(0.149)	0.766	1.351
Feels NHS has Improved:				
Conservative	0.400	(0.121)	0.162	0.637
Labour	−0.175	(0.130)	−0.429	0.079
Liberal Democrat	0.083	(0.164)	−0.239	0.405
Income:				
Conservative	0.094	(0.034)	0.027	0.161
Labour	−0.041	(0.036)	−0.112	0.029
Liberal Democrat	0.050	(0.045)	−0.039	0.138
Female:				
Conservative	0.687	(0.237)	0.223	1.152
Labour	0.575	(0.249)	0.087	1.064
Liberal Democrat	0.691	(0.320)	0.065	1.318
Age:				
Conservative	0.021	(0.008)	0.005	0.037
Labour	−0.017	(0.008)	−0.033	−0.001
Liberal Democrat	0.011	(0.011)	−0.010	0.032
Constant:				
Conservative	−3.891	(0.740)	−5.341	−2.440
Labour	−0.574	(0.723)	−1.990	0.843
Liberal Democrat	−5.016	(1.005)	−6.985	−3.046
Number of Individuals	890			
Number of Choice Alternatives	3,560			

Note: All alternative specific coefficients are relative to the UKIP.

the other choice categories, the choice probabilities may not uniformly increase or decrease as the independent variable increases.

As the value of an alternative specific variable increases for one category of the dependent variable, the choice probability for that category will uniformly increase if the coefficient on that variable is positive, and will uniformly decrease if the coefficient on that variable is negative, with the choice probabilities for all other categories moving in the opposite direction.

Multinomial logit models have a property known as the *independence of irrelevant alternatives* (IIA). For any two choice alternatives j and h, the ratio of choice probabilities is:

$$\frac{\exp(X_{ij}\beta + A_i\gamma_j)}{\sum_{k=1}^{J}\exp(X_{ik}\beta + A_i\gamma_k)} \Big/ \frac{\exp(X_{ih}\beta + A_i\gamma_h)}{\sum_{k=1}^{J}\exp(X_{ik}\beta + A_i\gamma_k)} = \frac{\exp(X_{ij}\beta + A_i\gamma_j)}{\exp(X_{ih}\beta + A_i\gamma_h)}. \quad (25)$$

The relative odds of selecting alternative j over alternative h do not depend on which other alternatives are available, or the characteristics of any other alternatives in the model – that is, all other alternatives are assumed to be irrelevant to the choice between these two alternatives.

5.2 First Differences

For two different sets of values for the independent variables X_A and X_B (which can include both alternative specific and alternative invariant variables), the first difference for choice category j in a multinomial logit model is calculated as:

$$\Delta p_j(X_A \to X_B) = \Pr(y = j|X_B) - \Pr(y = j|X_A), \quad (26)$$

where the choice probability $\Pr(y = j|X)$ is defined in Equation 24. For alternative specific variables, first differences are typically calculated by changing the value of the variable for just one of the choice alternatives.

Returning to the vote choice example described above, I calculated the substantive effect of a change in a hypothetical voter's approval of EU membership from "neither approve nor disapprove" to "disapprove" through a first difference. I began by creating two different hypothetical cases, one with a neutral view of British membership in the EU ("neither approve nor disapprove"), and one with a disapproving view ("disapprove"). All other variables were held constant across both hypothetical cases – the alternative invariant variables were held at their medians, and the alternative specific distance on the tax/spend scale was held at the median for each party across voters.[28] I then calculated predicted probabilities for each of the four parties for both hypothetical cases, with uncertainty in these probabilities calculated using the method of simulated coefficients with 1000 draws. The first difference was then calculated as the difference between the predicted probabilities

---

[28] The hypothetical case in this example was a 54-year-old male, thought that the National Health Service got a little worse since the 2010 General Election, had an income between £26,000 and £31,199, and perceived a distance of 2 units on the tax/spend scale between his ideal point and the position of each political party.

Table 12 First differences in vote choice based on approval of British membership in the European Union

	Median	**(se)**	**95% CI**	
Conservative				
Neutral	0.401	(0.030)	0.342	0.459
Disapprove	0.373	(0.034)	0.307	0.439
Neutral → Disapprove	−0.028	(0.017)	−0.062	0.005
Labour				
Neutral	0.362	(0.029)	0.309	0.420
Disapprove	0.263	(0.029)	0.212	0.321
Neutral → Disapprove	−0.098	(0.015)	−0.129	−0.068
Liberal Democrat				
Neutral	0.077	(0.014)	0.053	0.107
Disapprove	0.052	(0.013)	0.031	0.084
Neutral → Disapprove	−0.024	(0.006)	−0.038	−0.012
UKIP				
Neutral	0.157	(0.023)	0.119	0.207
Disapprove	0.308	(0.032)	0.245	0.374
Neutral → Disapprove	0.150	(0.020)	0.113	0.189

Note: Estimates were based on the multinomial logit model presented in Table 11. Standard errors and confidence intervals were calculated using 1000 sets of simulated coefficients.

for each choice category. Since approval of EU membership is an alternative invariant variable, the first differences for each choice category may be either positive or negative, except for the largest and smallest values of the alternative specific coefficients. Table 12 presents the results from the predicted probability and first difference calculations across the 1000 simulated coefficients.

As expected, when views of British membership in the EU changed from neutral to disapproving, the probability of voting for the UKIP increased, and the probability of voting for the Labour and Liberal Democrat parties decreased. The 95% confidence intervals on the changes for these three parties did not overlap zero, demonstrating that these probability changes were statistically significant at the 5% level. The decline in the probability of voting for the Conservative party as the hypothetical voter became more disapproving of EU membership was not statistically significant at the 5% level – this is perhaps unsurprising, as the Conservative party had also expressed "Eurosceptic" views before the 2015 election.

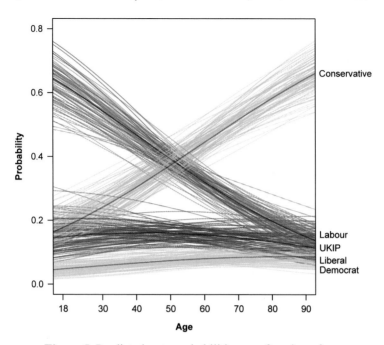

Figure 5 Predicted vote probabilities as a function of age

Another example of a first difference calculation for an alternative invariant variable is demonstrated in Figure 5, which presents the changes in the predicted probabilities from the multinomial logit model in Table 11 as age varies, holding all other independent variables at their median values.[29] Uncertainty in these probabilities was calculated using the method of simulated coefficients with 1000 draws. All 1000 predicted probability curves generated from the 1000 sets of simulated coefficients are presented for each choice category, with the probability curves for the mean of the draws presented as a darker line.

The alternative specific coefficient on age is largest for the Conservative Party and smallest for the Labour Party, so as age increased, the choice probability uniformly increased for the Conservative Party and uniformly decreased for the Labour Party. For the other choice categories, the choice probabilities were not guaranteed to uniformly increase or decrease as age increased.

---

[29] The hypothetical case in this example was male, neither approved nor disapproved of British membership in the European Union, thought that the National Health Service got a little worse since the 2010 General Election, had an income between £26,000 and £31,199, and perceived a distance of 2 units on the tax/spend scale between his ideal point and the position of each political party.

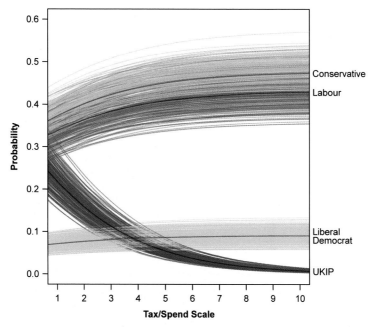

Figure 6 Predicted vote probabilities as a function of distance on the
tax/spend scale to the UKIP

First differences can also be calculated for alternative specific variables.
An example is demonstrated in Figure 6, which presents the changes in the
predicted probabilities from the multinomial logit model in Table 11 as the
distance between the hypothetical voter and the UKIP on the tax/spend scale
varies, holding all other variables at their median values.[30] Uncertainty in these
probabilities was calculated using the method of simulated coefficients with
1000 draws. All 1000 predicted probability curves generated from the 1000
sets of simulated coefficients are presented for each choice category, with the
probability curves for the mean of the draws presented as a darker line.

The coefficient on distance on the tax/spend scale is negative, so as the distance between the UKIP and the hypothetical voter on this scale increased,
the choice probability for the UKIP decreased, and the choice probabilities
for all other parties increased. The effect of the IIA assumption is apparent in
Figure 6. While changing distance on the tax/spend scale for the UKIP affects
the absolute probabilities for each alternative and the relative odds for selecting

---

[30] The hypothetical case in this example was a 54-year-old male, neither approved nor disapproved
of British membership in the European Union, thought that the National Health Service got a
little worse since the 2010 General Election, and had an income between £26,000 and £31,199.

the UKIP over the other alternatives, the relative odds for the other three parties in the model remain unchanged.[31]

Finally, I demonstrate a first difference based on changes in the choice probabilities across the entire sample. To estimate the substantive effect of public opinion on EU membership on the election outcome in Great Britain, I calculated the predicted share of voters who supported each party based on the observed values of the independent variables, and compared it to a counterfactual scenario under which public opinion about EU membership was more negative. More negative opinions on EU membership were simulated by randomly selecting one-quarter of the voters in the sample, and shifting the values on the EU approval variable for these voters down to the next lowest category (randomly selected voters already in the lowest category of approval were not shifted).[32] I applied sample enumeration with the appropriate sample weights to both scenarios, multiplied the estimated shares by 100 in order to express them as percentages, and accounted for statistical uncertainty using the method of simulated coefficients with 1000 draws. These results are presented in Table 13.

The predicted vote shares based on the observed sample are quite close to the actual vote shares among the subset of voters in Great Britain who voted for one of the four major parties, which were 41.9% Conservative, 34.7% Labour, 9.0% Liberal Democrat, and 14.3% UKIP (Hawkins, Keen, and Nakatudde 2015). The first difference calculation shows that if public opinion on British membership in the EU had been more negative, the vote share for the UKIP would have increased, while the vote shares for the other three parties would have decreased (although the change in the Conservative vote share was not statistically significant at the 5% level).

5.3 Marginal Effects and Elasticities

As with ordered choice models, each of the J choice categories in an multinomial choice model will have a separate marginal effect or elasticity, which gives the slope of the tangent line to each of the J probability curves at some given values of the independent variables.

---

[31] Across the entire range of the tax/spend scale, the relative odds of voting Conservative over Labour were always 1.07, the relative odds of voting Conservative over Liberal Democrat were always 5.20, and the relative odds of voting Labour over Liberal Democrat were always 4.88.

[32] The counterfactual shift for each category in the approval of EU membership variable changed "strongly disapprove" from 13.7% to 19.3% of voters, "disapprove" from 22.0% to 21.6% of voters, "neither approve nor disapprove" from 19.2% to 21.2% of voters, "approve" from 32.2% to 28.6% of voters, and "strongly approve" from 12.8% to 9.4% of voters.

Table 13 Predicted vote shares based on shifts in public opinion on membership in the European Union

	Median	**(se)**	**95% CI**	
Conservative				
Observed EU Opinions	42.864	(1.451)	39.910	45.880
Negative EU Opinions	42.683	(1.466)	39.680	45.588
Observed → Negative	−0.223	(0.280)	−0.754	0.349
Labour				
Observed EU Opinions	34.205	(1.370)	31.468	36.879
Negative EU Opinions	32.877	(1.353)	30.314	35.447
Observed → Negative	−1.355	(0.261)	−1.871	−0.833
Liberal Democrat				
Observed EU Opinions	8.784	(0.964)	7.052	10.968
Negative EU Opinions	8.280	(0.928)	6.611	10.330
Observed → Negative	−0.511	(0.160)	−0.820	−0.196
UKIP				
Observed EU Opinions	14.000	(1.036)	12.120	16.237
Negative EU Opinions	16.081	(1.146)	13.938	18.619
Observed → Negative	2.076	(0.239)	1.616	2.546

Note: Estimates were based on the multinomial logit model presented in Table 11, and are displayed as percentages. Standard errors and confidence intervals were calculated using 1000 sets of simulated coefficients.

For an alternative invariant variable a_v, the marginal effects for choice category j in a multinomial logit model are given by:

$$\frac{\partial p_j}{\partial a_v} = p_j \left[\gamma_{jv} - \sum_{k=1}^{J} p_k \gamma_{kv} \right]. \tag{27}$$

The marginal effects of an alternative invariant variable will always be positive for the choice category with the largest coefficient on the variable, will always be negative for the choice category with the smallest coefficient on the variable, and will sum to zero across the choice categories.

For an alternative specific variable x_{jv} there are two different types of marginal effects. The first is the change in the choice probability for an alternative given a change in the value of an alternative specific variable of interest for the same alternative. This is known as a *direct marginal effect*. The second is the change in the choice probability for an alternative given a change in the value of the alternative specific variable of interest for a different alternative. This is known as a *cross-marginal effect*. For instance, a direct marginal effect would be the change in the probability of voting for the Labour Party given a change in the tax/spend scale difference for the Labour Party, while a cross-marginal effect would be the change in the probability of voting for the Labour Party given a change in the tax/spend scale difference for the Conservative party. Cross-marginal effects are only relevant for alternative specific variables, since changing the value of an alternative invariant variable directly affects all choice categories.

The direct marginal effect for choice alternative j for a change in an alternative specific variable x_{jv} is given by:

$$\frac{\partial p_j}{\partial x_{jv}} = \beta_v p_j (1 - p_j), \tag{28}$$

while the cross-marginal effect for choice alternative j for a change in an alternative specific variable x_{hv} for choice alternative h is given by:

$$\frac{\partial p_j}{\partial x_{hv}} = -\beta_v p_j p_h. \tag{29}$$

The marginal effect for a change in an alternative specific variable for a choice category will have the same sign as the coefficient on the variable, while the cross-marginal effects will have the opposite sign. The marginal effect and associated cross-marginal effects for a single change in an alternative specific variable will sum to zero.

As with the other discrete choice models discussed previously, the marginal effect of an independent variable will depend both on the particular value of that variable and on the values of the other independent variables. Marginal effects are typically reported as the weighted average of the marginal effects across all individuals in the sample (the AME), or the marginal effect calculated at the sample mean (the MEM).

The relative influence of two different alternative specific independent variables on the choice probabilities can be determined through the ratio of their marginal effects:

$$\frac{\partial p_j}{\partial x_{jv}} \frac{\partial p_j}{\partial x_{jz}} = \left(\beta_v p_j (1 - p_j) \right) / \left(\beta_z p_j (1 - p_j) \right) = \beta_v / \beta_z. \tag{30}$$

The ratio of coefficients reveals the change in x_{jz} that would be required in order to produce the same change in the choice probability for category j as a 1-unit change in x_{jv}. Substituting the cross-marginal effect from Equation 29 in for the direct marginal effect reveals that this same ratio also holds for changes in alternative specific independent variables for choice categories other than category j.

Note that this simple interpretation does not apply if one or both of the variables being considered is alternative invariant – substituting the marginal effects for one or two alternative invariant variables into Equation 30 demonstrates that in this case the change in one variable required to produce the same change in the choice probability for a category as a 1-unit change in another variable does not reduce to a simple ratio of coefficients. Thus, ratios of coefficients are usually only considered for alternative specific variables.

The elasticity of an alternative invariant variable a_v for choice category j is given by:

$$\frac{\partial p_j / p_j}{\partial a_v / a_v} = \frac{\partial p_j}{\partial a_v} \frac{a_v}{p_j} = p_j \left[\gamma_{jv} - \sum_{k=1}^{J} p_k \gamma_{kv} \right] \frac{a_v}{p_j} = a_v \left[\gamma_{jv} - \sum_{k=1}^{J} p_k \gamma_{kv} \right]. \quad (31)$$

Note that unlike the marginal effects for alternative invariant variables, the elasticities on alternative invariant variables will not necessarily sum to zero across the choice categories.

The elasticity for choice alternative j for a change in an alternative specific variable x_{jv} is given by:

$$\frac{\partial p_j / p_j}{\partial x_{jv} / x_{jv}} = \frac{\partial p_j}{\partial x_{jv}} \frac{x_{jv}}{p_j} = \beta_v p_j (1 - p_j) \frac{x_{jv}}{p_j} = \beta_v x_{jv} (1 - p_j), \quad (32)$$

while the cross-elasticity for choice alternative j for a change in the value of an alternative specific variable x_{hv} for choice alternative h is given by:

$$\frac{\partial p_j / p_j}{\partial x_{hv} / x_{hv}} = \frac{\partial p_j}{\partial x_{hv}} \frac{x_{hv}}{p_j} = -\beta_v p_j p_h \frac{x_{hv}}{p_j} = -\beta_v x_{hv} p_h. \quad (33)$$

Unlike the marginal effect and associated cross-marginal effects, the elasticity and associated cross-elasticities for a single change in an alternative specific variable will not necessarily sum to zero. Note that the cross-elasticities for the choice alternatives $j \neq h$ only depend on the characteristics of choice alternative h, meaning that a change in the value of an alternative specific variable for choice alternative h will change the probabilities of all of the other choice alternatives by the same percentage. This restriction on the substitution patterns between choice alternatives is due to the IIA property of the MNL mentioned earlier. As with marginal effects, elasticities are usually calculated as the weighted average of the elasticities for all observations (average elasticity), or calculated at the sample mean (elasticity at the mean).

Table 14 presents the marginal effects and elasticities related to approval of British membership in the European Union (an alternative invariant variable). Uncertainty on these substantive effects was estimated using the method of simulated coefficients with 1000 draws.

Table 14 Marginal effects and elasticities related to approval of British membership in the European Union and vote choice

	Median	(se)	95% CI	
Conservative				
AME	0.006	(0.012)	−0.016	0.030
MEM	−0.018	(0.017)	−0.050	0.016
Average Elasticity	−0.004	(0.130)	−0.243	0.246
Elasticity at the Mean	−0.119	(0.115)	−0.335	0.105
Labour				
AME	0.055	(0.010)	0.033	0.073
MEM	0.070	(0.016)	0.038	0.100
Average Elasticity	0.741	(0.158)	0.428	1.048
Elasticity at the Mean	0.625	(0.152)	0.337	0.929
Liberal Democrat				
AME	0.022	(0.008)	0.008	0.037
MEM	0.025	(0.009)	0.009	0.043
Average Elasticity	0.958	(0.313)	0.373	1.596
Elasticity at the Mean	0.847	(0.309)	0.261	1.461
UKIP				
AME	−0.082	(0.009)	−0.099	−0.065
MEM	−0.077	(0.008)	−0.092	−0.063
Average Elasticity	−2.280	(0.301)	−2.872	−1.704
Elasticity at the Mean	−2.398	(0.311)	−3.026	−1.818

Note: Estimates were based on the multinomial logit model presented in Table 11. Standard errors and confidence intervals were calculated using 1000 sets of simulated coefficients.

As expected based on the coefficients on approval of EU membership in Table 11, the marginal effect of this variable is positive for the choice alternative with the largest coefficient (the Liberal Democrats), and negative for the choice alternative with the smallest coefficient (the UKIP – recall the coefficients on the alternative invariant variables are assumed to be zero for this choice category). Also note that the median estimates of the marginal effects sum to zero (subject to rounding error) across the choice categories. The calculated marginal effects and elasticities for approval of British membership in the EU were relatively large for the UKIP, which is unsurprising given the importance of this issue to the UKIP campaign. For instance, the average marginal effects suggest that the effect of a 1-unit increase in the approval of EU membership scale reduced the probability of voting for the UKIP by about 0.08,

Table 15 Marginal effects and elasticities related to distance on the tax/spend scale for the UKIP and vote choice

	Median	(se)	95% CI	
UKIP				
AME	−0.038	(0.003)	−0.045	−0.031
MEM	−0.035	(0.005)	−0.045	−0.026
Average Elasticity	−0.943	(0.078)	−1.086	−0.788
Elasticity at the Mean	−0.931	(0.077)	−1.073	−0.778
Conservative				
Average Cross-Marginal Effect	0.021	(0.002)	0.017	0.025
Cross-Marginal Effect at the Mean	0.018	(0.003)	0.014	0.024
Average Cross-Elasticity	0.091	(0.009)	0.074	0.108
Cross-Elasticity at the Mean	0.102	(0.015)	0.075	0.136
Labour				
Average Cross-Marginal Effect	0.014	(0.001)	0.011	0.016
Cross-Marginal Effect at the Mean	0.013	(0.002)	0.010	0.017
Average Cross-Elasticity	0.091	(0.009)	0.074	0.108
Cross-Elasticity at the Mean	0.102	(0.015)	0.075	0.136
Liberal Democrat				
Average Cross-Marginal Effect	0.003	(0.001)	0.002	0.005
Cross-Marginal Effect at the Mean	0.004	(0.001)	0.003	0.005
Average Cross-Elasticity	0.091	(0.009)	0.074	0.108
Cross-Elasticity at the Mean	0.102	(0.015)	0.075	0.136

Note: Estimates were based on the multinomial logit model presented in Table 11. Standard errors and confidence intervals were calculated using 1000 sets of simulated coefficients.

while the average elasticities suggest that a 1% increase on this scale reduced the probability of voting for the UKIP by about 2.3%.

The marginal effects and elasticities related to a change in the distance on the tax/spend scale for the UKIP (an alternative specific variable), as well as the associated cross-marginal effects and cross-elasticities, are presented in Table 15. Uncertainty on these substantive effects was estimated using the method of simulated coefficients with 1000 draws.

The coefficient on the tax/spend scale in Table 11 was negative, so the marginal effects and elasticities for a change in this variable for the UKIP are negative, while the cross-marginal effects and cross-elasticities are positive. The median estimates of the marginal effects and cross-marginal effects sum to zero (subject to rounding error) across the choice categories.

Due to the IIA property of the multinomial logit, the cross-elasticities for the Conservative, Labour, and Liberal Democrat parties are equal, whether calculated on average or at the mean. Note that the elasticities presented in Table 15 are individual-level elasticities – while the IIA property guarantees the individual-level cross-elasticities will be equal, this is not generally true for the aggregate cross-elasticities calculated through probability weighted sample enumeration (see Section 3.2).

Overall, these results indicate a somewhat inelastic relationship between distance on the tax/spend scale and vote choice. For example, the average elasticity indicates that a 1% increase in distance on the tax/spend scale reduced the probability of voting for the UKIP by about 0.9%, while increasing the probability of voting for each of the other three parties by 0.1%. As usual, the marginal effects and elasticities in Tables 14 and 15 are best interpreted as the expected effect from a very small increase in the independent variable.

5.4 Odds Ratios

It is possible to calculate odds for any two groupings of categories of the dependent variable in a multinomial logit model, but the odds most typically considered are the odds of observing one choice alternative versus another. If the dependent variable has J choice categories, there will be $(J(J - 1))/2$ pairwise comparisons of choice categories for which odds could be calculated. The odds of selecting choice alternative j versus choice alternative h are given in Equation 25. Odds ratios can be calculated based on these odds for both alternative specific and alternative invariant variables.

For alternative specific variables, the odds ratios do not depend on which two choice categories are considered. Following from Equations 18 and 25, the change in the odds of observing $y = j$ versus $y = h$ resulting from a 1-unit increase in an alternative specific variable x_v for alternative j is given by:

$$OR(x_{jv} \rightarrow x_{jv} + 1)$$
$$= \frac{\exp((x_{jv} + 1)\beta_v + X_{j-v}\beta_{-v} + A\gamma_j)}{\exp(x_{hv}\beta_v + X_{h-v}\beta_{-v} + A\gamma_h)} \bigg/ \frac{\exp(x_{jv}\beta_v + X_{j-v}\beta_{-v} + A\gamma_j)}{\exp(x_{hv}\beta_v + X_{h-v}\beta_{-v} + A\gamma_h)}$$
$$= \exp(\beta_v). \tag{34}$$

Thus, for alternative specific variables in a multinomial logit model, odds ratios can be calculated by simply multiplying the coefficient by whatever δ-unit change in the independent variable is of interest, and then exponentiating.

Since the coefficients on alternative invariant variables vary across choice categories, the odds ratios will depend on which two choice categories are being compared. The odds ratios calculated on alternative invariant variables are sometimes referred to as *conditional odds ratios* or *relative risk ratios* for this reason. Again following from Equations 18 and 25, the change in the odds of observing $y = j$ versus $y = h$ for a 1-unit increase in an alternative invariant variable a_v is given by:

$$
\begin{aligned}
OR(a_v \to a_v + 1) \\
= \frac{\exp(X_{ij}\beta + (a_v + 1)\gamma_{jv} + A_{-v}\gamma_{j-v})}{\exp(X_{ih}\beta + (a_v + 1)\gamma_{hv} + A_{-v}\gamma_{h-v})} \Big/ \frac{\exp(X_{ij}\beta + a_v\gamma_{jv} + A_{-v}\gamma_{j-v})}{\exp(X_{ih}\beta + a_v\gamma_{hv} + A_{-v}\gamma_{h-v})} \\
= \frac{\exp(\gamma_{jv})}{\exp(\gamma_{hv})} = \exp(\gamma_{jv} - \gamma_{hv}).
\end{aligned}
\tag{35}
$$

Thus, for alternative invariant variables in a multinomial logit model, odds ratios can be calculated by simply calculating the difference in the alternative specific coefficients for choice categories j and h, multiplying by whatever δ-unit change in the independent variable is of interest, and then exponentiating. If choice alternative h is the baseline category in the multinomial logit model so that $\gamma_{hv} = 0$, this simplifies the calculation to $\exp(\gamma_{jv}\delta)$.

Table 16 presents the odds ratios associated with a 1-unit change in each of the independent variables. Median odds ratios, standard errors and 95% confidence intervals were calculated using the method of simulated coefficients.

For the alternative specific tax/spend scale, the odds ratio reveals that the odds of voting for a party decreased as the distance between a voter and a party on the tax/spend scale increased by 1 unit. The odds ratios for the alternative invariant variables demonstrate how a 1-unit increase in these variables affected the odds of voting for the Conservative, Labour, and Liberal Democrat parties relative to the UKIP. For example, the odds of voting for the Conservative party over the UKIP more than doubled if an individual increased by one unit on the "Approves of Britain in the EU" scale, and the odds of voting for Labour or the Liberal Democrats over the UKIP nearly tripled. Odds ratios for the alternative invariant variables for other pairwise comparisons of parties can be calculated using the formula in Equation 35 – for example, an increase of one unit on the "Approves of Britain in the EU" scale increased the odds of voting for the Labor party over the Conservative party by a factor of approximately 1.3 (from the coefficients in Table 11, this is calculated as $\exp(0.986 - 0.743)$).

6 Substantive Effects in Mixed Discrete Choice Models

Finally, I consider the interpretation of mixed discrete choice models. The mixed discrete choice models considered here are of the form:

$$
p_{ij} = \Pr(y_i = j | X_{ij}, Z_{ij}) = \int_\eta F(X_{ij}\beta + Z_{ij}\eta_i)g(\eta)d\eta,
\tag{36}
$$

Table 16 Odds ratios in the multinomial logit model for vote choice in the
2015 British General Election

Independent Variable	Median	(se)	95% CI	
Difference on Tax/Spend	0.675	(0.022)	0.634	0.718
Approves of Britain in EU:				
Conservative	2.102	(0.233)	1.692	2.612
Labour	2.679	(0.313)	2.130	3.370
Liberal Democrat	2.882	(0.431)	2.151	3.863
Feels NHS has Improved:				
Conservative	1.491	(0.181)	1.176	1.891
Labour	0.839	(0.109)	0.651	1.082
Liberal Democrat	1.086	(0.178)	0.787	1.499
Income:				
Conservative	1.099	(0.038)	1.028	1.175
Labour	0.960	(0.034)	0.894	1.030
Liberal Democrat	1.051	(0.047)	0.962	1.148
Female:				
Conservative	1.988	(0.471)	1.250	3.163
Labour	1.778	(0.443)	1.091	2.898
Liberal Democrat	1.997	(0.638)	1.067	3.737
Age:				
Conservative	1.021	(0.008)	1.005	1.037
Labour	0.983	(0.008)	0.967	0.999
Liberal Democrat	1.011	(0.011)	0.990	1.033
Number of Individuals	890			
Number of Choice Alternatives	3,560			

Note: All odds ratios on alternative invariant variables are relative to the UKIP. Estimates were based on the multinomial logit model presented in Table 11. Median odds ratios, standard errors and confidence intervals were calculated using 1000 sets of simulated coefficients.

where y_i is the discrete dependent variable, $\Pr(y_i = j)$ is the probability that individual i selects choice category j, $X_{ij}\beta$ is a linear function of independent variables and fixed coefficients, and $F(.)$ is one of the discrete choice models described earlier. $Z_{ij}\eta_i$ is also a linear function of independent variables and coefficients, but unlike the fixed value of β, η follows a random distribution over individuals given by $g(\eta)$. The choice probability $\Pr(y_i = j)$ is obtained by integrating over this random distribution. The probability in Equation 36 is a weighted average of the discrete choice model probability $F(.)$ at various values of η_i, with the weights given by the probability distribution $g(\eta)$. Mixed models are so named because they are a "mixture" of alternative versions of the discrete choice model, each with different values of η. The distribution $g(\eta)$ is known as the mixing distribution. In some contexts, mixed models are known as *generalized linear mixed models (GLMM)*, *random coefficients models*, or *random effects models*.[33]

Two examples of mixed discrete choice models are presented in this section. The first is a *random effects logit* that examines how support for Scottish independence changed over time, while also accounting for unobserved individual characteristics that might lead Scottish voters to be more or less supportive of independence across all waves of a panel survey. The estimation and interpretation of mixed discrete choice models is explained in some detail through this example, which reveals that the interpretative techniques covered in earlier sections can also be applied to mixed discrete choice models in a straightforward way. A second example presents a *mixed multinomial logit* (more simply known as a *mixed logit*) that examines the choice of shoreline recreation sites in the San Francisco Bay Area in the aftermath of the *Cosco Busan* oil spill, while also accounting for unobserved heterogeneity in sensitivity to travel costs and preferences for the various recreation sites. Many other examples of mixed discrete choice models exist or could be developed; the interpretative techniques described here will also apply to these models.

6.1 Example: A Random Effects Logit Model of the Effect of Brexit on Support for Scottish Independence

On September 18, 2014, Scottish voters[34] participated the Scottish Independence Referendum, which posed the question: "Should Scotland be an independent country?" and 55.3% voted "no" (McInnes, Ayers, and Hawkins 2014). A central concern during the referendum campaign was whether an independent Scotland would remain a member of the European Union.

Less than two years later (on June 23, 2016), the European Union Referendum was held in the UK. That referendum posed the question: "Should the United Kingdom remain a member of the European Union or leave the European Union?" and 51.9% of UK voters voted "leave." However, in Scotland there was strong support for remaining in the EU, with 62.0% voting "remain"

---

[33] Some researchers refer to models that contain both fixed and random coefficients as "mixed models." To avoid confusion, I apply this term to all models that are a mixture of discrete choice models, whether some or all of the coefficients are random.

[34] Eligibility to vote in the Scottish Independence Referendum was based on eligibility to vote in Scottish Parliamentary and local elections.

(Uberoi 2016). Here I consider whether the Brexit referendum result changed the preferences of pro-EU Scottish voters for an independent Scotland.

The data for this example come from the British Election Study Internet Panel (Fieldhouse et al. 2015). They consist of 1,178 individuals who participated in three waves of the panel study: (1) immediately following the Scottish Independence Referendum (between September 19 and October 17, 2014), (2) immediately following the 2015 British General Election (between May 8 and May 26, 2015), and (3) immediately following the European Union Referendum (between June 24 and July 4, 2016).

The dependent variable in this example is support for Scottish independence. In each survey wave, survey respondents were asked how they would vote if there was another referendum on Scottish independence, with a vote to leave the UK ("yes") coded as a 1, and a vote to remain in the UK ("no") coded as a 0.

I modeled support for Scottish independence as a function of several independent variables. The key independent variable came from a survey question that asked respondents how they would vote if there was a referendum on Britain's membership in the European Union, with a "remain in the EU" vote coded as a 1, and a "leave the EU" vote coded as a 0. A dummy variable for the post-Brexit wave of the survey (1 = post-Brexit, 0 = pre-Brexit) was also included in the model, as was the interaction between the post-Brexit variable and the EU referendum variable. This interaction term was intended to capture any change in the effect of pro-EU attitudes on preferences for Scottish independence after the Brexit vote. I expected that individuals who wished to remain in the EU would become more supportive of Scottish independence after Brexit.

Several other individual characteristics were also included in the model. Respondents were asked to rate their satisfaction with the way democracy worked in Scotland on a four-point scale, with higher numbers indicating greater satisfaction.[35] I expected greater satisfaction with democracy in Scotland would lead respondents to be more likely to support Scottish independence. Respondents were also asked to assess their personal likelihood of unemployment over the next year on a five-point scale, with higher numbers indicating a greater fear of unemployment.[36] Due to the potential for economic and political uncertainty that would result from the establishment of an independent Scotland, I expected that respondents with a greater fear of

---

[35] The categories on this satisfaction scale were "very dissatisfied," "a little dissatisfied," "fairly satisfied," and "very satisfied."

[36] The categories on this likelihood of unemployment scale were "very unlikely," "fairly unlikely," "neither likely nor unlikely," fairly likely," and "very likely."

unemployment would be less likely to support Scottish independence. The model also included place of birth (Scotland = 1, all other places = 0) – I expected native Scots would be more likely to support Scottish independence.

Since each individual in the survey provided multiple responses, *unobserved heterogeneity* may have influenced the choice probabilities. For instance, it was possible that an independent Scotland might decide not to retain the Queen of England as head of state, and instead become a republic. Thus, an individual's affection for (or dislike of) the British monarchy might make this individual less (or more) likely to support Scottish independence across all waves of the survey. However, these types of influences were unobserved.

The effect of this unobserved heterogeneity on the choice probabilities can be addressed with a random effects logit. For individual i at time t, the probability of choosing $y = 1$ is given by:

$$\Pr(y_{it} = 1 | X_{it}, \alpha_i) = \Lambda(X_{it}\beta + \alpha_i), \tag{37}$$

where α_i are the unobserved effects that lead each individual to be more or less likely to select $y = 1$ (Scottish independence). If α_i was observed, it could simply enter Equation 37 as a constant term when calculating the logit choice probability. That is, conditional on the value of α_i, the random effects logit model is simply a binary logit.

However, the value of α_i is unobserved. In order to solve for the unconditional choice probability, the choice probability must be integrated over the distribution of α, which in this case is assumed to be a normal distribution with mean zero and a variance to be estimated ($\alpha \sim N(0, \sigma_\alpha^2)$). This integration yields a weighted average of simple binary logit probabilities:

$$\Pr(y_{it} = 1 | X_{it}) = \int_\alpha \Lambda(X_{it}\beta + \alpha)\phi(\alpha)d\alpha. \tag{38}$$

In general, the integrals in mixed models do not have a closed form.[37] Thus, in order to estimate the unconditional choice probabilities, the integral must be approximated. This is done by selecting R possible values of the random coefficients, calculating the conditional choice probabilities for each value, and calculating a weighted average of the conditional choice probabilities. For the random effects logit the approximation of the unconditional choice probabilities is given by:

$$p_{it} = \Pr(y_{it} = 1 | X_{it}, v_r, \omega_r) = \sum_{r=1}^{R} [\Lambda(X_{it}\beta + v_r\sigma)]\,\omega_r, \tag{39}$$

---

[37] There are some examples of mixed models with closed form integrals, such as random effects linear regression and the negative binomial model for event count data.

where v_r is a value selected from a standard normal distribution ($v \sim N(0, 1)$), ω_r is the weight for that value, and σ is an additional coefficient to be estimated. Larger values of σ indicate greater amounts of unobserved heterogeneity.

The values of v_r and ω_r can be determined in two ways. One approach is *quadrature*, which approximates the integral over the mixing distribution with an interpolation function. The values of v_r and ω_r are determined by the quadrature nodes and associated weights from the interpolation function. The simplest method of quadrature approximates the integral of a function g by choosing evenly spaced nodes across the domain of the mixing distribution, with the weight of each node determined by $g(v_r)$ – this is known as the rectangle rule or a Reimann sum. In the case of the random effects logit with a normally distributed random effect, the nodes and weights are usually determined through *Gauss-Hermite quadrature*, which approximates the integral with the "probabilist" version of a Hermite polynomial (Press et al. 2007, Ch. 4).[38]

The other approach is *simulation*, which approximates the integral over the mixing distribution g by taking a large number of random draws from the mixing distribution. The values of v_r are simply the values drawn from the mixing distribution, with each draw given equal weight. In many cases the draws will be based on quasi-random sequences (such as Halton sequences) that create a more even spread of points across the domain of the mixing distribution in comparison to random draws, allowing for more accurate approximation of the integral with fewer draws (Press et al. 2007, ch. 7). Since estimation time is based in part on the number of draws used to approximate the integral, the use of such *quasi-random draws* can greatly speed estimation time (Train 2009, ch. 9).

Table 17 presents two different estimates of a random effects logit model on the Scottish referendum data. The first estimates the random effect using quadrature (with 64 quadrature points), while the second uses simulation (with 500 Halton draws). A simple binary logit model is also presented in Table 17 – this model is also known as a "pooled" logit model, since it treats the data as a pooled set of cross-sections rather than panel data.

Note that quadrature and simulation produce nearly identical results – both approaches approximate the same integral, and both become more accurate as the number of draws increases. The results differ for the pooled logit, which

---

[38] Note that most tables and functions for quadrature provide the "physicist" versions of the Gauss-Hermite quadrature points – to convert these to the "probabilist" versions, multiply the nodes by $\sqrt{2}$ and divide the weights by π. Also note that many applications use adaptive quadrature, under which additional nodes can be added to regions of the function in which approximation error is expected to be high. For clarity of exposition, in this example I use nonadaptive quadrature.

Table 17 Logit models for supporting Scottish independence

Random Effects Logit (Quadrature)				
Independent Variable	**Coefficient**	**(se)**	**95% CI**	
Wants to Remain in EU	0.717	(0.376)	−0.019	1.453
Post-Brexit Survey Wave	−2.196	(0.363)	−2.907	−1.485
Remain in EU × Post Brexit	4.214	(0.482)	3.270	5.158
Satisfied with Scottish Democracy	1.371	(0.156)	1.066	1.677
Perceived Risk of Unemployment	0.386	(0.118)	0.154	0.618
Born in Scotland	3.000	(0.671)	1.684	4.316
Constant				
Mean of Coefficient	−7.730	(0.756)	−9.213	−6.248
Std. Dev. of Coefficient	6.662	(0.515)	5.653	7.671

Random Effects Logit (Simulation)				
Independent Variable	**Coefficient**	**(se)**	**95% CI**	
Wants to Remain in EU	0.703	(0.263)	0.189	1.218
Post-Brexit Survey Wave	−2.213	(0.397)	−2.991	−1.434
Remain in EU × Post Brexit	4.223	(0.545)	3.155	5.291
Satisfied with Scottish Democracy	1.371	(0.138)	1.100	1.642
Perceived Risk of Unemployment	0.384	(0.085)	0.218	0.551
Born in Scotland	3.000	(0.318)	2.377	3.623
Constant				
Mean of Coefficient	−7.649	(0.635)	−8.893	−6.404
Std. Dev. of Coefficient	6.655	(0.510)	5.655	7.654

Pooled Logit				
Independent Variable	**Coefficient**	**(se)**	**95% CI**	
Wants to Remain in EU	0.574	(0.100)	0.378	0.769
Post-Brexit Survey Wave	−0.398	(0.151)	−0.693	−0.103
Remain in EU × Post Brexit	0.746	(0.180)	0.393	1.100
Satisfied with Scottish Democracy	0.899	(0.046)	0.808	0.990
Perceived Risk of Unemployment	0.316	(0.032)	0.252	0.379
Born in Scotland	0.635	(0.092)	0.455	0.815
Constant	−3.999	(0.180)	−4.352	−3.646
Number of Individuals	1,178			
Number of Choices	3,534			

Note: The quadrature model was estimated with 64 quadrature points. The simulation model was estimated with 500 Halton draws.

assumes there is no unobserved heterogeneity. The examples of interpretation here are based on the random effects logit model estimated using quadrature.

The interpretation of the coefficients in a random effects logit is the same as for a binary logit, with positive coefficients indicating that as the value of the independent variable increases, p_{it} increases, and negative coefficients indicating the opposite. While the interpretation of discrete choice models with interaction terms can be complicated (Ai and Norton 2003), in a difference-in-difference model such as this the treatment effect (in this case, the effect of Brexit on individuals who wanted to remain in the EU) is simply represented by the coefficient on the interaction term (Karaca-Mandic, Norton, and Dowd 2012; Puhani 2012). These results indicate that after Brexit, individuals who wished to remain in the EU became more supportive of Scottish independence, while those who wished to leave the EU became less supportive (the dummy variable for the post-Brexit survey wave is negative, while the interaction between this dummy variable and the dummy variable indicating a desire to remain in the EU is positive). The magnitude of this divergence of opinion is made clear using first differences in Table 18 below. The results in Table 17 also demonstrate that greater satisfaction with Scottish democracy, higher perceived risks of unemployment, and Scottish birth all increased the probability that an individual would have supported Scottish independence.

Although the coefficients of the pooled logit and the random effects logit appear similar in Table 17, the probability curves produced by these models differ substantially. This is demonstrated in Figure 7, which presents the changes in predicted probabilities from both the random effects logit and the pooled logit in Table 17 for a single hypothetical case as the level of satisfaction with Scottish democracy varies, with all other variables held constant at their median values.[39] Uncertainty in these probabilities was calculated using the method of simulated coefficients with 1000 draws. All 1000 predicted probability curves generated from the 1000 sets of simulated coefficients are presented for each choice category, with the probability curves for the mean of the draws presented as a darker line.

Figure 7 also presents the probability curves from a random effects logit model that holds the random effect at its mean ($\alpha_i = 0$). The probability curve obtained by holding the random effect constant is sometimes known as a *subject-specific* probability, and is the probability curve if the value of the random effect for a subject was known. The unconditional random effects

---

[39] This hypothetical individual wanted to remain in the EU, was interviewed pre-Brexit, felt the likelihood of personal unemployment in the next year was "fairly unlikely," and was born in Scotland.

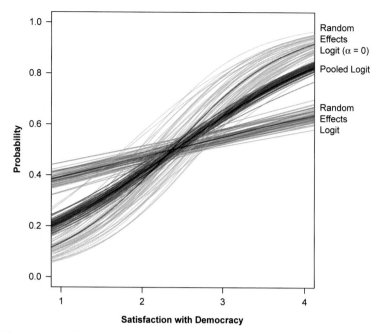

Figure 7 Predicted probabilities of supporting Scottish independence as a function of satisfaction with Scottish democracy

logit probability curve is obtained by averaging over all of the possible subject-specific probability curves (by integrating over the distribution of the random effects), and is thus sometimes known as a *population-averaged* probability. As Figure 7 makes clear, simply setting the random effect to its mean does not yield the same probability curve as integrating over the random effects – the population-averaged probability curve is attenuated relative to the subject-specific probability curve. Note that while the unconditional probability curve for the random effects logit in some cases will resemble a logit curve, it is not in fact a logit.

6.1.1 First Differences

For two different sets of values for the independent variables (X_A and X_B), the first difference for choice category j in a random effects logit model is calculated as:

$$\Delta p(X_A \rightarrow X_B) = \Pr(y = 1|X_B, v_r, \omega_r) - \Pr(y = 1|X_A, v_r, \omega_r), \tag{40}$$

where the unconditional choice probability $\Pr(y = 1|X)$ is defined in Equation 39. The same values of v_r and ω_r should be used for both X_A and X_B to ensure the first difference is not affected by simulation noise.

Table 18 First differences in the predicted probability of supporting Scottish independence

	Median	**(se)**	**95% CI**	
Wants to Remain in EU				
Pre-Brexit	0.550	(0.018)	0.516	0.588
Post-Brexit	0.663	(0.018)	0.628	0.697
Pre-Brexit → Post-Brexit	0.113	(0.013)	0.088	0.140
Wants to Leave EU				
Pre-Brexit	0.509	(0.021)	0.467	0.551
Post-Brexit	0.383	(0.024)	0.337	0.430
Pre-Brexit → Post-Brexit	−0.125	(0.019)	−0.163	−0.089
Difference Between First Differences	0.238	(0.023)	0.192	0.285

Note: Estimates were based on the random effects logit model estimated using quadrature presented in Table 17. Confidence intervals were calculated using 1000 sets of simulated coefficients.

I calculated the first differences between the pre- and post-Brexit survey waves for two different hypothetical individuals, one who wished to remain in the EU, and one who did not. All other variables were held constant at their medians across both hypothetical cases.[40] The difference between the first differences was also calculated, and uncertainty was accounted for using the method of simulated coefficients with 1000 draws. Table 18 presents the results from the predicted probability, first difference, and difference in differences calculations across the 1000 simulated coefficients.

As expected, after the Brexit decision, individuals who wished to remain in the EU became significantly more likely to support Scottish independence, while individuals who wished to leave the EU became significantly less likely to support Scottish independence. The difference between these first differences was also statistically significant at the 5% level, indicating that in the wake of the Brexit referendum, preferences for Scottish independence diverged based on the desire to remain in or leave the EU.

---

[40] This hypothetical individual was "fairly satisfied" with the way democracy worked in Scotland, was interviewed pre-Brexit, felt the likelihood of personal unemployment in the next year was "fairly unlikely," and was born in Scotland.

Table 19 Marginal effects and elasticities related to satisfaction with democracy and supporting Scottish independence

	Median	**(se)**	**95% CI**	
Average Marginal Effect (AME)	0.073	(0.009)	0.057	0.092
Marginal Effect at the Mean (MEM)	0.078	(0.010)	0.060	0.099
Average Elasticity	0.404	(0.050)	0.311	0.509
Elasticity at the Mean	0.424	(0.057)	0.321	0.545

Note: Estimates were based on the random effects logit model estimated with quadrature presented in Table 17. Standard errors and confidence intervals were calculated using 1000 sets of simulated coefficients.

6.1.2 Marginal Effects and Elasticities

The unconditional probability curve for the random effects logit is not a logit, so simply applying the formula for the marginal effect of a logit to this curve is incorrect. Instead, the marginal effects for the random effects logit associated with a change in independent variable x_v are calculated as the weighted average of the logit marginal effects for each value of v_r:

$$\frac{\partial p}{\partial x_v} = \sum_{r=1}^{R} [\Lambda(X_{it}\beta + v_r\sigma)(1 - \Lambda(X_{it}\beta + v_r\sigma))\beta_v]\omega_r. \tag{41}$$

As usual, these marginal effects are most often calculated as the average marginal effect across all individuals in the sample (the AME) or at the sample mean (the MEM).

After calculating marginal effects, elasticities can be calculated in the same way as for a simple binary logit, by multiplying the marginal effect by x_v/p, where p is the unconditional choice probability given by Equation 39 (note the elasticity is not calculated for each value of v_r and then averaged).

Table 19 presents the marginal effects and elasticities related to satisfaction with Scottish democracy. Uncertainty on these substantive effects was estimated using the method of simulated coefficients with 1000 draws.

Since satisfaction with democracy has a positive coefficient, all of these substantive effects are also positive. These results indicate a somewhat inelastic relationship between satisfaction with Scottish democracy and the probability of supporting Scottish independence. For example, the average elasticity indicates that a 1% increase in distance on the satisfaction with Scottish democracy scale increased the probability of supporting Scottish independence by about 0.4%. As usual, the marginal effects and elasticities in Table 19 are best interpreted as the expected effect from a very small increase in the independent variable.

6.1.3 Odds Ratios

Two different types of odds ratios can be calculated for mixed discrete choice models. One type is based on the conditional choice probabilities, and is often known as the *subject-specific odds ratio*. The subject-specific odds ratio is interpreted as the change in the odds related to a change in the value of a variable for a specific individual, conditional on the value of the random effect. If X_B is identical to X_A, except that x_v is increased by 1 unit, then following from Equations 18 and 37 the subject-specific odds ratio that results from changing from from X_A to X_B in a random effects logit model is:

$$OR_{ss}(X_A \rightarrow X_B) = \frac{\Pr(y_{it} = 1|X_{itB}, \alpha_i)}{1 - \Pr(y_{it} = 1|X_{itB}, \alpha_i)} \Big/ \frac{\Pr(y_{it} = 1|X_{itA}, \alpha_i)}{1 - \Pr(y_{it} = 1|X_{itA}, \alpha_i)} = \exp(\beta_v).$$

$$(42)$$

Although the value of the random effect is unknown, it is treated as a constant term in this calculation, so it cancels out of the odds ratio calculation. Thus, subject-specific odds ratios for the random effects logit model can be calculated in the same way as the odds ratios for a binary logit, by simply multiplying the coefficient by whatever δ-unit change in the independent variable is of interest and then exponentiating.

The other type of odds ratio that can be calculated for a mixed discrete choice models is based on the unconditional choice probabilities, and is often known as the *population-averaged odds ratio*. The population-averaged odds ratio is interpreted as the change in the odds resulting from a change in the value of an independent variable across the entire population. If X_B is identical to X_A, except that x_v is increased by 1 unit, then the population-averaged odds ratio that results from changing from from X_A to X_B in a random effects logit model is:

$$OR_{pa}(X_A \rightarrow X_B) = \frac{\Pr(y_{it} = 1|X_{itB}, v_r, \omega_r)}{1 - \Pr(y_{it} = 1|X_{itB}, v_r, \omega_r)} \Big/ \frac{\Pr(y_{it} = 1|X_{itA}, v_r, \omega_r)}{1 - \Pr(y_{it} = 1|X_{itA}, v_r, \omega_r)}.$$

$$(43)$$

Note that the integration over the random effects in the unconditional choice probabilities prevents the simple calculation of odds ratios as seen for the discrete choice models discussed earlier. The values of all of the independent variables will matter when calculating population odds ratios. As with first differences, the same values of v_r and ω_r should be used for both X_A and X_B to ensure this odds ratio is not affected by simulation noise.

Population-averaged odds ratios in mixed discrete choice models can be calculated by first estimating the unconditional choice probabilities, and then computing the odds ratio directly. For the random effects logit the unconditional choice probabilities are given by in Equation 39. Another approach specific to the random effects logit is to estimate the coefficient values that describe the cumulative logistic approximation of the population-averaged probability curve, and then exponentiate these population-averaged (or "marginalized") coefficients.[41]

The subject-specific and population-averaged odds ratios for this example are given in Table 20. Uncertainty on these substantive effects was estimated using the method of simulated coefficients with 1000 draws.

The subject-specific odds ratios are larger in magnitude than the population-averaged odds ratios, as expected based on the population-averaged and subject-specific probability curves in Figure 7. The population-averaged odds ratios were calculated as the sample-weighted mean odds ratio for each draw of simulated coefficients, assuming each variable increases by 1 unit from its actual value. Note that the interaction term in this model complicated the calculation of the odds ratios (Norton, Wang, and Ai 2004).[42]

6.2 Example: A Mixed Logit Model of Shoreline Recreation in the San Francisco Bay Area

On November 7, 2007, the 68,000-ton container ship *Cosco Busan* struck a tower of the San Francisco-Oakland Bay Bridge in heavy fog. The collision ruptured two of the ship's fuel tanks, spilling more than 53,000 gallons of oil into the San Francisco Bay. Wind and tides pushed the oil ashore at many sites

---

[41] Most researchers interested in obtaining population-averaged coefficients estimate them directly through the generalized estimating equation (GEE) approach (Liang and Zeger 1986). However, several methods for approximating population-averaged coefficients from mixed discrete choice model results have been proposed. For the random effects logit, Zeger, Liang, and Albert (1988) approximate the population-averaged coefficients as $\beta_{pa} \approx \beta / \sqrt{(1 + c^2\sigma^2)}$), where β are the coefficients from the random effects logit, σ is the estimated standard deviation of the unobserved heterogeneity, and $c = 16\sqrt{3}/15\pi$. Hedeker et al. (2018) approximate the population-averaged coefficients as $\beta_{pa} \approx (X'_{it}X_{it})^{-1}X'_{it}\ln(p_{it}/(1 - p_{it}))$, where p_{it} are the unconditional choice probabilities from the random effects logit. Both of these approximations proved to be fairly accurate for the example presented here.

[42] The odds ratio associated with wanting to remain in the EU is conditional on whether the survey took place pre- or post-Brexit. The subject-specific odds ratio for the pre-Brexit survey waves was calculated by exponentiating the coefficient on *Wants to Remain in EU*, while the population-averaged odds ratio was calculated by incrementing this variable by 1 unit. The subject-specific odds ratio for the post-Brexit survey wave was calculated by exponentiating the sum of the coefficients on *Wants to Remain in EU*, *Post-Brexit Survey Wave*, and *Remain in EU × Post Brexit*, while the population-averaged odds ratio was calculated by incrementing all three of these variables by 1 unit.

Table 20 Odds ratios in the random effects logit model for supporting Scottish independence

Subject-Specific Odds Ratios				
Independent Variable	**Median**	**(se)**	**95% CI**	
Wants to Remain in EU				
Post-Brexit Survey Wave = 0	2.052	(0.827)	0.989	4.199
Post-Brexit Survey Wave = 1	15.514	(6.929)	6.538	32.513
Post-Brexit Survey Wave	0.111	(0.040)	0.055	0.226
Satisfied with Scottish Democracy	3.961	(0.630)	2.929	5.3469
Perceived Risk of Unemployment	1.466	(0.177)	1.165	1.845
Born in Scotland	19.079	(20.744)	5.367	79.305

Population-Averaged Odds Ratios				
Independent Variable	**Median**	**(se)**	**95% CI**	
Wants to Remain in EU				
Post-Brexit Survey Wave = 0	1.187	(0.110)	1.012	1.420
Post-Brexit Survey Wave = 1	1.915	(0.196)	1.590	2.370
Post-Brexit Survey Wave	0.593	(0.049)	0.503	0.692
Satisfied with Scottish Democracy	1.387	(0.060)	1.282	1.512
Perceived Risk of Unemployment	1.094	(0.032)	1.040	1.161
Born in Scotland	2.037	(0.302)	1.527	2.740
Number of Individuals	1,178			
Number of Choices	3,534			

Note: Estimates were based on the random effects logit model estimated with quadrature presented in Table 17. The population-averaged odds ratios were calculated as the mean odds ratios in the sample for a 1-unit increase in the independent variable. Standard errors and confidence intervals were calculated using 1000 sets of simulated coefficients.

in San Francisco Bay and along the Pacific Coast. In addition to the significant damage to wildlife, shoreline habitat, and fisheries, the spill temporarily closed many Bay Area beaches to recreational use. As one part of a comprehensive Natural Resource Damage Assessment (NRDA), the *Cosco Busan* trustees[43] undertook a survey examining shoreline recreation site choice in the San Francisco Bay Area (Cosco Busan Oil Spill Trustees 2012).

    The data for this example come from a telephone survey of 1,312 San Francisco Bay Area residents conducted between June and August, 2008 (English

---

[43] Government agencies acting on behalf of the public as trustees for natural resources.

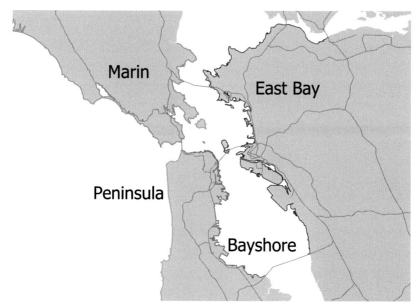

Figure 8 Shoreline recreation regions in the San Francisco Bay Area

2010). The survey respondents identified 110 different shoreline recreation sites that they had visited on day trips within the last three months. I aggregated these shoreline recreation sites into four regions: Marin, the East Bay, Bayshore, and the Peninsula. These shoreline recreation regions are presented in Figure 8.[44]

The dependent variable in this example is the choice of region for shoreline recreation. Of the 1,312 survey respondents, 690 reported taking between one and six shoreline recreation trips to at least one of the four regions in Figure 8, while 622 reported taking no shoreline recreation trips (the "no trip" option). There was a total of 1,844 choices in the data.

I modeled the choice of region for shoreline recreation as a function of two alternative specific independent variables. The first was each respondent's travel cost to each of the four recreational regions. Travel costs were calculated as the average round-trip driving distance between the respondent's residence and the shoreline recreation sites in each region, times 54.1 cents per

---

[44] The Marin region is defined as the coast of Marin County between Dillon Beach (on the Pacific coast, north of the area represented in Figure 8) and the mouth of Gallinas Creek in San Francisco Bay. The East Bay region is defined as the coasts of Contra Costa and Alameda Counties between the Benicia-Martinez Bridge in the north and the San Mateo Bridge in the south. The Bayshore region is defined as the coasts of San Mateo and San Francisco Counties between the San Mateo Bridge in the south and the Golden Gate Bridge in the north. The Peninsula region is defined as the coasts of San Mateo and San Francisco Counties between the Golden Gate Bridge and Pescadero State Beach (on the Pacific coast, south of the area represented in Figure 8).

mile (American Automobile Association 2008), plus bridge tolls. The travel cost for the "no trip" alternative was of course zero. Travel costs are often used to quantify damages to recreational opportunities caused by environmental disasters such as the *Cosco Busan* spill, as one measure of the value of a recreational trip is the amount of money an individual was willing to spend to take the trip. The second was the average number of bridge crossings required when driving between the respondent's residence and each of the shoreline recreation sites in each region.[45] Alternative specific constants for the recreational regions were also included, with the "no trip" alternative as the baseline category.

As with the random effects logit example in Section 6.1, each individual in the survey provided multiple responses, so unobserved heterogeneity is likely to influence the choice probabilities. For example, respondents are expected to be less likely to visit recreational regions that have greater travel costs, but individual sensitivity to travel costs may vary for unobserved reasons, leading to random variation in the travel cost coefficient across respondents. Unobserved heterogeneity in this context is sometimes known as *taste variation*.

The effect of this unobserved heterogeneity on the choice probabilities can be addressed with a mixed logit. Given the values of the random coefficients β_i, the probability that individual i chooses alternative j in choice scenario t is given by:

$$\Pr(y_{it} = j | X_{ijt}, \beta_i) = \frac{\exp(X_{ijt}\beta_i)}{\sum_{k=1}^{J} \exp(X_{ikt}\beta_i)}, \tag{44}$$

where X_{ikt} can contain both alternative specific and alternative invariant variables. Conditional on the values of the random coefficients β_i, the mixed logit model is simply a multinomial logit. Since the value of β_i is unobserved, integration over the distribution of β is required in order to solve for the unconditional choice probabilities. This integration yields a weighted average of simple multinomial logit probabilities:

$$\Pr(y_{it} = j | X_{ijt}) = \int_{\beta} \frac{\exp(X_{ijt}\beta_i)}{\sum_{k=1}^{J} \exp(X_{ikt}\beta_i)} g(\beta) d\beta, \tag{45}$$

---

[45] Depending on the location of the respondent's residence, the shortest route to different sites within a shoreline recreation region could involve a different number of bridge crossings – for instance, the shortest distance between a residence in the East Bay and the Marin shoreline recreation region could involve one or two bridge crossings, depending on the particular location of the shoreline recreation site. See Figure 8.

where $g(\beta)$ is the joint distribution of the random coefficients. In this example, the coefficients on the alternative specific constants were specified as independent normal distributions, such that the coefficient for a particular individual could be positive or negative, since respondents may like or dislike a particular shoreline recreational region for unobserved reasons (e.g., ease of parking, quality of fishing). Similarly, the coefficient on bridge crossings was also specified as an independent normal distribution, as adding a bridge crossing to a trip might be viewed by some individuals as a positive (e.g., aesthetically pleasing views), and by others as a negative (e.g., an increased chance of traffic congestion). The coefficient on travel cost was specified as a lognormal distribution with a sign change, such that this coefficient is always negative. The use of lognormal distributions of this type for cost and price variables is common in mixed logit models – since the range of the lognormal distribution does not include zero, this prevents divide-by-zero problems when using the randomly distributed travel cost coefficient in willingness to pay (WTP) calculations (see the discussion around Equation 12 and Daly, Hess, and Train 2011).

As quadrature tends to become less accurate as the dimension of integration (the number of random coefficients) increases, the integrals in mixed logits are most commonly approximated via simulation. The approximation of the unconditional choice probabilities is given by:

$$p_{ijt} = \Pr(y_{it} = j | X_{ijt}, v_r, \omega_r) = \sum_{r=1}^{R} \left[\frac{\exp(X_{ijt}\beta + X_{ijt}v_r\sigma)}{\sum_{k=1}^{J} \exp(X_{ikt}\beta + X_{ikt}v_r\sigma)} \right] \omega_r, \qquad (46)$$

where v_r are values selected from the appropriate distribution for each random coefficient with mean zero and variance 1, ω_r is the weight for that set of draws (usually equal to $1/R$), and σ are additional coefficients describing $g(\beta)$ to be estimated (usually the standard deviations of the random coefficients).

Table 21 presents the results of estimating the mixed logit model described previously, using 500 Halton draws to simulate the integrals.

The interpretation of the coefficients in a mixed logit model is the same as that for a multinomial logit model. However, since the coefficients are random, the effect of a variable on the choice probabilities will vary across individuals. In the case of travel cost, the entire support for the distribution of the coefficient is negative, so increasing travel cost to a recreational region reduces the probability of visiting that region, with the reduction in probability for a given increase in travel cost varying across individuals. For the normally distributed coefficients, different signs for different individuals are possible. For

Table 21 Mixed logit model for shoreline recreation choice in the San Francisco Bay Area

Independent Variable	Coefficient	(se)	95% CI	
Travel Cost				
Mean of ln(Coefficient)	−0.965	(0.159)	−1.276	−0.655
Std. Dev. of ln(Coefficient)	3.400	(0.584)	2.257	4.544
Bridge Crossings:				
Mean of Coefficient	−2.048	(0.395)	−2.823	−1.273
Std. Dev. of Coefficient	1.085	(0.606)	−0.103	2.273
Constant:				
Marin				
Mean of Coefficient	6.819	(1.105)	4.654	8.985
Std. Dev. of Coefficient	1.128	(0.381)	0.382	1.874
East Bay				
Mean of Coefficient	5.052	(1.041)	3.011	7.092
Std. Dev. of Coefficient	0.700	(0.505)	−0.291	1.691
Bayshore				
Mean of Coefficient	6.186	(1.099)	4.031	8.341
Std. Dev. of Coefficient	0.068	(2.370)	−4.578	4.713
Peninsula				
Mean of Coefficient	7.711	(1.130)	5.496	9.925
Std. Dev. of Coefficient	0.356	(0.460)	−0.546	1.259
Number of Individuals	1,312			
Number of Choices	1,844			
Number of Choice Alternatives	9,220			

Note: The alternative specific constants for each region were estimated relative to no trip. All random coefficients followed normal distributions except travel cost, which followed a lognormal distribution with a sign change (the coefficients for travel cost are for the underlying normal distribution on the negative of travel cost; to obtain the lognormal travel cost distribution, exponentiate and multiply by −1). Random coefficients were estimated using 500 Halton draws.

example, the normally distributed random coefficient on bridge crossings has a mean of −2.048 and a standard deviation of 1.085, indicating that while respondents were less likely to travel to a shoreline recreation region as more of the sites in that region required crossing a bridge, for a small minority of respondents ($\approx$ 3%) increased bridge crossings had the opposite effect (although note the estimated standard deviation of the bridge crossings coefficient was not statistically significant at the 5% level).

6.2.1 First Differences

For two different sets of values for the independent variables (X_A and X_B), the first difference for choice category j in a mixed logit model is calculated as:

$$\Delta p_j(X_A \rightarrow X_B) = \Pr(y = j | X_B, v_r, \omega_r) - \Pr(y = j | X_A, v_r, \omega_r), \tag{47}$$

where the unconditional choice probability $\Pr(y = j | X)$ is defined in Equation 46. As with the random effects logit, the same values of v_r and ω_r should be used for both X_A and X_B to ensure the first difference is not affected by simulation noise. First differences based on changes in the choice probabilities across the entire sample can be calculated by applying sample enumeration to the unconditional choice probabilities.

Table 22 presents an estimate of the substantive effect of a hypothetical shoreline closure due to an oil spill during the time covered by the trustee's survey. The predicted share of individuals who selected each recreation region or the "no trip" alternative in the sample were compared to a counterfactual scenario under which the East Bay region was closed to shoreline recreation. The counterfactual scenario under which the East Bay region was closed was created by setting the alternative specific constant for that region to a large negative number, shifting the choice probabilities for all individuals for that region to (approximately) zero. I applied sample enumeration with the appropriate sample weights to both scenarios, multiplied the estimated shares by 100 in order to express them as percentages, and accounted for statistical uncertainty using the method of simulated coefficients with 1000 draws.

Under this counterfactual scenario, the closure of the East Bay region due to the hypothetical oil spill would have led most individuals who had intended to travel to the East Bay to move their shoreline recreation trips to other regions (most frequently the Peninsula), while others would have canceled their shoreline recreation trips. Related "lost trip" calculations are often used in natural resource damage assessments and other analyses of counterfactual scenarios (e.g., English 2010; Glasgow and Train 2018; Small and Rosen 1981).

6.2.2 Marginal Effects and Elasticities

Marginal effects for the mixed logit are calculated as the weighted mean of the marginal effects calculated for each draw of v_r. For example, the direct marginal effect for choice alternative j for a change in an alternative specific variable x_{jv} in a mixed logit is given by:

$$\frac{\partial p_j}{\partial x_{jv}} = \sum_{r=1}^{R} \beta_{vr} p_{jr} (1 - p_{jr}) \omega_r, \tag{48}$$

Table 22 First differences in predicted share of trips based on closure of the East Bay Region due to spill

	Median	**(se)**	**95% CI**	
Marin				
East Bay Open	7.878	(0.847)	6.196	9.410
East Bay Closed	9.336	(1.000)	7.343	11.145
Open → Closed	1.448	(0.217)	1.050	1.878
East Bay				
East Bay Open	9.568	(1.058)	7.400	11.471
East Bay Closed	0	(0.000)	0	0
Open → Closed	−9.568	(1.058)	−11.471	−7.400
Bayshore				
East Bay Open	14.235	(2.960)	10.888	21.419
East Bay Closed	16.241	(2.795)	12.541	22.849
Open → Closed	1.885	(0.369)	1.150	2.590
Peninsula				
East Bay Open	19.440	(1.467)	16.418	21.980
East Bay Closed	22.949	(1.785)	19.501	25.981
Open → Closed	3.513	(0.542)	2.415	4.512
No Trip				
East Bay Open	48.159	(1.472)	45.741	51.585
East Bay Closed	50.812	(1.536)	48.508	54.559
Open → Closed	2.707	(0.417)	2.058	3.658

Note: Estimates based on the mixed logit model presented in Table 21, and are presented as percentages. Standard errors and confidence intervals were calculated using 1000 sets of simulated coefficients.

where p_{jr} is the choice probability conditional on v_r. Cross-marginal effects and direct marginal effects for alternative invariant variables are calculated in the same way.

After calculating marginal effects, elasticities can be calculated in the same way as for a multinomial logit, by multiplying the marginal effect by x_{jv}/p_j, where p_j is the unconditional choice probability given by Equation 46 (note the elasticity is not calculated for each draw of v_r and then averaged).

The marginal effects and elasticities related to a change in the travel cost to the East Bay region (an alternative specific variable), as well as the associated cross-marginal effects and cross-elasticities, are presented in Table 23. Uncertainty on these substantive effects was estimated using the method of simulated coefficients with 1000 draws.

Table 23 Marginal effects and elasticities related to travel cost to the East Bay Region and shoreline recreation choice

	Median	**(se)**	**95% CI**	
East Bay				
AME ($\times 10^2$)	−0.453	(0.081)	−0.635	−0.327
MEM ($\times 10^2$)	−0.262	(0.058)	−0.409	−0.173
Average Elasticity	−0.858	(0.167)	−1.243	−0.610
Elasticity at the Mean	−1.491	(0.282)	−2.092	−1.017
Marin				
Average Cross-Marginal Effect ($\times 10^2$)	0.027	(0.006)	0.018	0.041
Cross-Marginal Effect at the Mean ($\times 10^2$)	0.017	(0.005)	0.010	0.030
Average Cross-Elasticity	0.060	(0.014)	0.042	0.094
Cross-Elasticity at the Mean	0.048	(0.016)	0.029	0.090
Bayshore				
Average Cross-Marginal Effect ($\times 10^2$)	0.076	(0.016)	0.046	0.114
Cross-Marginal Effect at the Mean ($\times 10^2$)	0.079	(0.031)	0.029	0.147
Average Cross-Elasticity	0.148	(0.058)	0.054	0.274
Cross-Elasticity at the Mean	0.118	(0.064)	0.030	0.258
Peninsula				
Average Cross-Marginal Effect ($\times 10^2$)	0.075	(0.016)	0.051	0.108
Cross-Marginal Effect at the Mean ($\times 10^2$)	0.117	(0.029)	0.073	0.186
Average Cross-Elasticity	0.097	(0.022)	0.066	0.150
Cross-Elasticity at the Mean	0.122	(0.035)	0.075	0.212
No Trip				
Average Cross-Marginal Effect ($\times 10^2$)	0.274	(0.049)	0.202	0.386
Cross-Marginal Effect at the Mean ($\times 10^2$)	0.049	(0.015)	0.026	0.085
Average Cross-Elasticity	0.078	(0.014)	0.056	0.109
Cross-Elasticity at the Mean	0.022	(0.006)	0.012	0.037

Note: Estimates were based on the mixed logit model presented in Table 21. Marginal effects were multiplied by 100 for ease of interpretation. Standard errors and confidence intervals were calculated using 1000 sets of simulated coefficients.

The coefficient on travel cost was constrained to be negative for all respondents, so the marginal effects and elasticities for a change on this variable for the East Bay region are negative, while the cross-marginal effects and cross-elasticities are positive. As with the multinomial logit, the median estimates of the marginal effects and cross-marginal effects for the mixed logit sum to zero (subject to rounding error). However, unlike the MNL the IIA property does not hold for the mixed logit, so the cross-elasticities are no longer constrained to be equal (Train 2009, p. 141). Overall, these results indicate a somewhat inelastic relationship between travel cost and the choice of region for shoreline recreation. For example, the average elasticity indicates that a 1% increase in travel cost to the East Bay region reduced the probability of visiting that region by about 0.9%, while increasing the probability of visiting the Bayshore region by proportionately more than the Marin and Peninsula regions. As usual, these marginal effects and elasticities are best interpreted as the expected effect from a very small increase in the independent variable.

As with a MNL, the relative influence of two different alternative specific independent variables on the choice probabilities in a mixed logit can be determined through the ratio of their marginal effects. If one or both of the variables has a random coefficient, this ratio will vary across individuals.

The distribution of the WTP for a bridge crossing was calculated as the ratio of the coefficient on bridge crossings to the coefficient on travel cost (multiplied by -1). I generated 500 values of each coefficient using Halton draws, and then calculated the ratio for every possible combination of the bridge crossings and travel cost coefficients, yielding a distribution based on a total of 250,000 WTPs. This method of calculating coefficient ratios is known as the "complete combinatorial" method (Poe, Giraud, and Loomis 2005). Uncertainty was estimated using the method of simulated coefficients with 1000 draws, producing 1000 different WTP distributions across individuals. The median WTP for a bridge crossing was $-\$4.20$ (95% CI: $-\$1.50$, $-\$7.92$) – that is, the average (median) individual would pay to avoid a bridge crossing.[46]

6.2.3 Odds Ratios

Population-averaged odds ratios for the mixed logit can be calculated using the unconditional choice probabilities evaluated at two different values for an independent variable, as described for the random effects logit. Unlike the multinomial logit, the IIA property does not hold for mixed logits, so the odds ratios

---

[46] Note that the mean of the WTP distribution tends to be heavily skewed when dividing by a lognormally distributed cost coefficient due to draws of the cost coefficient near zero. In this case, the mean WTP for a bridge crossing was $-\$656.79$, which is clearly unrealistic.

Table 24 Population-averaged odds ratios in the mixed logit model for shoreline recreation choice in the San Francisco Bay Area, relative to no trip

Independent Variable	Median	(se)	95% CI	
Travel Cost				
Marin	0.977	(0.004)	0.967	0.983
East Bay	0.967	(0.006)	0.953	0.975
Bayshore	0.949	(0.009)	0.930	0.964
Peninsula	0.973	(0.006)	0.959	0.980
Bridge Crossings				
Marin	0.863	(0.059)	0.712	0.932
East Bay	0.786	(0.071)	0.615	0.880
Bayshore	0.782	(0.068)	0.625	0.880
Peninsula	0.840	(0.065)	0.677	0.921
Number of Individuals	1,312			
Number of Choices	1,844			
Number of Choice Alternatives	9,220			

Note: The population-averaged odds ratios were calculated as the mean odds ratios in the sample for a 1-unit increase in the independent variable for all four shoreline recreation regions simultaneously. Median odds ratios, standard errors and confidence intervals were calculated using 1000 sets of simulated coefficients.

will differ for each pairwise comparison of alternatives, even for alternative specific variables.

Subject-specific odds ratios can be calculated for independent variables with fixed coefficients by simply exponentiating the coefficients. It is also possible to calculate subject-specific odds ratios for independent variables with random coefficients by selecting a value for the random coefficient, such as the mean – however, in most applications this would make little sense, since the true value of the random coefficient is unknown for each subject.

The population-averaged odds ratios for the shoreline recreation choice example are given in Table 24. The population-averaged odds ratios were calculated as the sample-weighted mean odds ratio for each region relative to the "no trip" alternative, assuming each variable increases by 1 unit from its actual value for all four shoreline recreation regions simultaneously. Median odds ratios, standard errors, and 95% confidence intervals were calculated using the method of simulated coefficients with 1000 draws. Subject-specific odds ratios are not presented because all coefficients in the mixed logit model were specified as random.

The population-averaged odds ratios in Table 24 demonstrate that both a $1 increase in travel cost and an increase in the average number of bridge crossings by 1 reduced the odds of taking a shoreline recreation trip for all regions relative to the "no trip" alternative.

7 Extensions

The basic techniques covered in this Element – first differences in predicted probabilities, marginal effects and elasticities, and odds ratios – can be applied to a wide variety of discrete choice models not discussed here, such as rank-ordered logits, generalized extreme value (GEV) models such as nested logits, and multinomial probits. These techniques can also be adapted to other types of models, such as event count models (e.g., Glasgow, Lewis, and Neiman 2012) – this Element provides a starting point for these extensions.

References

Agresti, Alan. 2013. *Categorical Data Analysis*. Third ed. Hoboken, NJ: John Wiley & Sons.

Ai, Chunrong and Edward C. Norton. 2003. "Interaction terms in logit and probit models." *Economics Letters* 80:123–129.

American Automobile Association. 2008. *Your Driving Costs: 2008 Edition*. Heathrow, FL: AAA Association Communication.

Ben-Akiva, Moshe and Steven R. Lerman. 1985. *Discrete Choice Analysis: Theory and Application to Travel Demand*. Cambridge, MA: The MIT Press.

Cosco Busan Oil Spill Trustees. 2012. *Oil Spill Final Damage Assessment and Restoration Plan/Environmental Assessment*. California Department of Fish and Game, California State Lands Commission, National Oceanic and Atmospheric Administration, United States Fish and Wildlife Service, National Park Service, Bureau of Land Management.

Daly, Andrew, Stephane Hess, and Kenneth Train. 2011. "Assuring finite moments for willingness to pay in random coefficient models." *Transportation* 39:19–31.

Davison, Anthony C. and David V. Hinkley. 1997. *Bootstrap Methods and Their Application*. New York: Cambridge University Press.

Diaconis, Persi and Bradley Efron. 1983. "Computer-intensive methods in statistics." *Scientific American* 248:116–130.

Dowd, Bryan E., William H. Greene, and Edward C. Norton. 2014. "Computation of standard errors." *Health Services Research* 49:731–750.

Easterly, William. 2006. *The White Man's Burden: Why the West's Efforts to Aid the Rest Have Done So Much Ill and So Little Good*. New York: Penguin Press.

Efron, Bradley and Gail Gong. 1983. "A leisurely look at the bootstrap, the jackknife, and cross-validation." *The American Statistician* 37:36–48.

Efron, Bradley and Robert J. Tibshirani. 1994. *An Introduction to the Bootstrap*. New York: Chapman & Hall.

English, Eric. 2010. *Cosco Busan Natural Resource Damage Assessment, Appendix J: Damage Estimate for Shoreline Recreation*. Boulder, CO: Stratus Consulting.

Fieldhouse, Ed, Jane Green, Geoff Evans, Hermann Schmitt, Cees van der Eijk, Jon Mellon, and Chris Prosser. 2015. *British Election Study: Internet Panel, Waves 1–13*. Manchester, UK: British Election Study.

Fieldhouse, Ed, Jane Green, Geoff Evans, Hermann Schmitt, Cees van der Eijk, Jon Mellon, and Chris Prosser. 2016. *British Election Study, 2015: Face-to-Face Post-Election Survey*. Manchester, UK: British Election Study.

Gelman, Andrew and Jennifer Hill. 2007. *Data Analysis Using Regression and Multilevel/Hierarchical Models*. New York: Cambridge University Press.

Glasgow, Garrett and Kenneth Train. 2018. "Lost use-value from environmental injury when visitation drops at undamaged sites." *Land Economics* 94:87–96.

Glasgow, Garrett, Matt Golder, and Sona Golder. 2012. "New empirical strategies for the study of parliamentary government formation." *Political Analysis* 20:248–270.

Glasgow, Garrett, Paul G. Lewis, and Max Neiman. 2012. "Local development policies and the foreclosure crisis in California: Can local policies hold back national tides?" *Urban Affairs Review* 48:64–85.

Greene, William H. and David A. Hensher. 2010. *Modeling Ordered Choices: A Primer*. New York: Cambridge University Press.

Hawkins, Oliver, Richard Keen, and Nambassa Nakatudde. 2015. "General Election 2015." *House of Commons Library Briefing Paper* CBP–7186:July 28, 2015. London: House of Commons.

Hedeker, Donald, Stephen du Toit, Hakan Demirtas, and Robert D. Gibbons. 2018. "A note on marginalization of regression parameters from mixed models of binary outcomes." *Biometrics* 74:354–361.

Hensher, David A., John M. Rose, and William H. Greene. 2015. *Applied Choice Analysis*. Second ed. Cambridge, UK: Cambridge University Press.

Herron, Michael. 1999. "Postestimation uncertainty in limited dependent variable models." *Political Analysis* 8:83–98.

Hole, Arne Risa. 2007. "A comparison of approaches to estimating confidence intervals for willingness to pay measures." *Health Economics* 16:827–840.

Karaca-Mandic, Pinar, Edward C. Norton, and Bryan Dowd. 2012. "Interaction terms in nonlinear models." *Health Services Research* 47:255–274.

Kiewiet, D. Roderick. 1983. *Macroeconomics and Micropolitics: The Electoral Effects of Economic Issues*. Chicago, IL: The University of Chicago Press.

Kinder, Donald R. and D. Roderick Kiewiet. 1981. "Sociotropic politics: The American case." *British Journal of Political Science* 11:129–162.

King, Gary, Michael Tomz, and Jason Wittenberg. 2000. "Making the most of statistical analyses: improving interpretation and presentation." *American Journal of Political Science* 44:347–361.

Krinsky, Itzhak and A. Leslie Robb. 1986. "On approximating the statistical properties of elasticities." *The Review of Economics and Statistics* 68: 715–719.

Krinsky, Itzhak and A. Leslie Robb. 1990. "On approximating the statistical properties of elasticities: A correction." *The Review of Economics and Statistics* 72:189–190.

Lewis-Beck, Michael S. 1988. *Economics and Elections*. Ann Arbor: University of Michigan Press.

Lewis-Beck, Michael S. and Martin Paldam. 2000. "Economic voting: An introduction." *Electoral Studies* 19:113–121.

Liang, Kung-Yee and Scott L. Zeger. 1986. "Longitudinal data analysis using generalized linear models." *Biometrika* 73:13–22.

Long, J. Scott. 1997. *Regression Models for Categorical and Limited Dependent Variables*. Thousand Oaks, CA: Sage Publications.

Louviere, Jordan J., David A. Hensher, and Joffre D. Swait. 2000. *Stated Choice Methods: Analysis and Application*. Cambridge, UK: Cambridge University Press.

Mandel, Micha. 2013. "Simulation-based confidence intervals for functions with complicated derivatives." *The American Statistician* 67:76–81.

Manski, Charles F. 1995. *Identification Problems in the Social Sciences*. Cambridge, MA: Harvard University Press.

McCullagh, Peter and John A. Nelder. 1989. *Generalized Linear Models*. Boca Raton, FL: Chapman & Hall/CRC.

McInnes, Roderick, Steven Ayers, and Oliver Hawkins. 2014. "Scottish Independence Referendum 2014." *House of Commons Library Briefing Paper* RP 14–50:September 30, 2014. London: House of Commons.

Norton, Edward C., Hua Wang, and Chunrong Ai. 2004. "Computing interaction effects and standard errors in logit and probit models." *The Stata Journal* 4:154–167.

Oehlert, Gary W. 1992. "A note on the delta method." *The American Statistician* 46:27–29.

Poe, Gregory L., Kelly L. Giraud, and John B. Loomis. 2005. "Computational methods for measuring the difference of empirical distributions." *American Journal of Agricultural Economics* 87:353–365.

Press, William H., Saul A. Teukolsky, William T. Vetterling, and Brian P. Flannery. 2007. *Numerical Recipes: The Art of Scientific Computing*. Third ed. New York: Cambridge University Press.

Puhani, Patrick A. 2012. "The treatment effect, the cross difference, and the interaction term in nonlinear "difference-in-differences" models." *Economics Letters* 115:85–87.

R Core Team. 2021. *R: A Language and Environment for Statistical Computing*. Vienna: R Foundation for Statistical Computing. www.R-project.org/

Sachs, Jeffrey. 2005. *The End of Poverty: Economic Possibilities for Our Time*. New York: Penguin Press.

Small, Kenneth A. and Harvey S. Rosen. 1981. "Applied welfare economics with discrete choice models." *Econometrica* 49:105–130.

The American National Election Studies (ANES). 2019. *ANES 2016 Time Series Study*. Ann Arbor, MI: Inter-university Consortium for Political and Social Research.

Train, Kenneth E. 2009. *Discrete Choice Methods with Simulation*. Second ed. New York: Cambridge University Press.

Uberoi, Elise. 2016. "European Union Referendum 2016." *House of Commons Library Briefing Paper* CBP–7639:June 29, 2016. London: House of Commons.

Uganda Bureau of Statistics. 2015. *Uganda Malaria Indicator Survey, 2014–2015*. Kampala, Uganda, and Rockville, MD: Uganda Bureau of Statistics and ICF International.

United Kingdom Independence Party. 2015. *Believe in Britain: UKIP Manifesto 2015*. Newton Abbot, UK: United Kingdom Independence Party.

Ver Hoef, Jay M. 2012. "Who invented the delta method?" *The American Statistician* 66:124–127.

Ward, Michael D. and John S. Ahlquist. 2018. *Maximum Likelihood for Social Science: Strategies for Analysis*. New York: Cambridge University Press.

Zeger, Scott L., Kung-Yee Liang, and Paul S. Albert. 1988. "Models for longitudinal data: A generalized estimating equation approach." *Biometrics* 44:1049–1060.

Cambridge Elements ☰

Quantitative and Computational Methods for the Social Sciences

R. Michael Alvarez

California Institute of Technology

R. Michael Alvarez has taught at the California Institute of Technology his entire career, focusing on elections, voting behavior, election technology, and research methodologies. He has written or edited a number of books (recently, *Computational Social Science: Discovery and Prediction* and *Evaluating Elections: A Handbook of Methods and Standards*) and numerous academic articles and reports.

Nathaniel Beck

New York University

Nathaniel Beck is Professor of Politics at NYU (and Affiliated Faculty at the NYU Center for Data Science) where he has been since 2003, before which he was Professor of Political Science at the University of California, San Diego. He is the founding editor of the quarterly *Political Analysis*. He is a fellow of both the American Academy of Arts and Sciences and the Society for Political Methodology.

About the Series

The Elements Series Quantitative and Computational Methods for the Social Sciences contains short introductions and hands-on tutorials to innovative methodologies. These are often so new that they have no textbook treatment or no detailed treatment on how the method is used in practice. Among emerging areas of interest for social scientists, the series presents machine learning methods, the use of new technologies for the collection of data, and new techniques for assessing causality with experimental and quasi-experimental data.

Cambridge Elements ☰

Quantitative and Computational Methods for the Social Sciences

Printed in the United States
by Baker & Taylor Publisher Services